P9-EDF-513

This special edition of the Food Writers' Favorites: Soups, Stews and Casseroles *is being offered to benefit MADD and help you better understand its work. Before enjoying the many recipes that follow, please take a few minutes to read over the material. It explains MADD's history and the services MADD performs. After reading these few pages, you will understand why MADD's work is so important. You will also learn how you can continue to support this worthwhile cause.*

It is estimated that two out of every five Americans will be involved in an alcohol-related crash in their lifetime. On average, 64 people die and 1,534 are injured each and every day as a result of alcohol and other drug-related driving crashes. Hopefully, through your support and involvement in the efforts of MADD, we can create a future that is less violent for us all.

Mothers Against Drunk Driving

"Mothers Against Drunk Driving mobilizes victims and their allies to establish the public conviction that drunk driving is unacceptable and criminal, in order to promote corresponding public policies, programs and personal accountability."

MADD was founded in California in 1980. An aggressive grassroots campaign resulted in California passing the toughest drunk driving laws in the country at that time.

This astounding success was only the beginning. Shortly thereafter, MADD grew into a nationwide, non-profit corporation with more than one million members and supporters. Today, thousands of concerned citizens are active volunteers in over 397 chapters in 48 states. Affiliates are active in Canada, Australia, New Zealand and Great Britain. MADD is made up of both women and men who share a common concern for safety on our roads.

Numerous successes fuel the MADD operation, both at the National Office in Texas and in states and communities scattered throughout America. Since 1980, more than 1,000 drunk driving laws have been enacted nationwide. The rights of victims and survivors of alcohol related crashes are now being viewed more equitably in a criminal justice system which, only a few years ago, made the rights of the intoxicated driver a priority. Youth programs affiliated with MADD have sprung up in almost every state, providing teenagers with a background in alcohol awareness and education.

MADD's Community Programs

MADD develops new ideas and programs to increase the unacceptability of drunk driving, and attempts to involve all Americans — especially our youth — in solving the problem. Some of our ongoing programs include:

Public Awareness Campaigns

Throughout the year, MADD conducts special campaigns to promote public awareness and raise the nation's consciousness of alcohol and other drug-impaired driving. These and other initiatives are MADD's most important tools for encouraging people to be responsible in their actions.

Project Red Ribbon: created by MADD to change the meaning of "tie one on" by asking drivers to tie a red ribbon to a visible location on their vehicles between Thanksgiving and New Year's Day. This is a simple but effective reminder to drive sober during the holiday season.

K.I.S.S. (Keep It a Safe Summer): spreads the word that summer months can be the most dangerous. A cornerstone of the program is the Family Vacation Pack, filled with safety tips and activities for the entire family!

Designated Driver: responsibility is the key to this program. The point: if you choose to drink, bring a friend who is not drinking to safely drive you home.

DRIVE FOR LIFE: is an annual public awareness campaign with one compelling goal...to save lives. MADD has selected one specific day—the Saturday of Labor Day Weekend—to focus increased education on the drunk driving issue. Citizens are asked to drive with their headlights on throughout that day in memory of the 64 men, women and children killed each day by drunk drivers and to sign a pledge not to drink and drive.

Candlelight Vigils: Each year MADD conducts Candlelight Vigils of Remembrance and Hope—remembrance of loved ones killed or injured in drunk driving crashes, and hope for a less violent future for us all.

Youth Education Programs

MADD has developed specific programs to reduce the prevalence of drinking and the incidence of drunk driving among America's youth. Components are designed to enhance student-parent dialogue, and to provide refusal skills training to show young people how to avoid dangerous situations involving alcohol and drug use.

Operation Prom/Graduation: This is a nationwide community awareness program that seeks to make prom and graduation nights memorable occasions, not memorial ones. Operation Prom/Graduation includes widespread alcohol- and drug-free activities and celebrations for students.

Nationwide Poster/Essay Contest: This national competition offers students in grades 1-12 the opportunity to exercise their creative writing and artistic skills to deliver a strong message about the dangers of drinking and driving. Individual entries compete at the National Office. The winners in each division then compete with organizational winners at the national level for awards and public recognition.

MADD Student Library: The Student Library is published annually to meet the needs of countless students who request information about teenage drunk driving. It contains statistics, case studies, articles on topics such as peer pressure and the legal aspects of teen drinking and an extensive bibliography of resources on highway safety issues. Educators and parents also regard it as a valuable resource.

Student Organizations: MADD offers guidance and detailed advice to high school students who are interested in organizing student groups to combat teenage impaired driving. Student leaders receive ideas for ongoing projects and programs to educate their peers and elevate their awareness about the disproportionate number of alcohol-related crashes caused by teenagers driving under the influence of alcohol and other drugs.

Friends Keep Friends Alive: MADD now offers an educational comic book directed at students in grades 4-9. The comic book teaches how to say no to drinking and drunk driving. It is offered in both English and Spanish.

FREE FOR LIFE: A refusal skills development program which teaches junior high school youth how to resist peer pressure to use alcohol and other drugs. The program relies on "peer education" techniques, having the students themselves plan and lead class discussions.

Speakers Bureaus

MADD chapters across America offer trained speakers to address civic and professional organizations, community groups, legislatures, public and private industries, schools and other concerned citizens. These knowledgeable leaders provide innovative lectures and educational information about critical traffic safety issues such as legislation, victims rights, community actions programs; and prevention techniques to remove intoxicated drivers from our highways.

Case/Court Monitoring

MADD's ongoing case/court monitoring program monitors the enforcement and legal process for DWI's in communities across America. Specifically, MADD volunteers monitor DWI arrests and cases being adjudicated in order to advise the public whether DWI laws, as well as enforcement, prosecution and defense are adequate.

MADD's Public Policy and Legislative Goals

Since 1980, tremendous progress has been made at both the state and federal levels in passing tougher anti-impaired driving legislation and regulations. However, as we begin a new decade, we see much more to be done. In the years ahead, MADD's mission will continue to focus on two primary goals: reducing alcohol- and other drug-impaired driving, and aiding victims of crashes caused by impaired driving—but with a renewed grass-roots drive, more organized, professional approach, and improved educational resources.

Reducing Impaired Driving: By the year 2000, MADD hopes to see a reduction in the proportion of alcohol-related traffic fatalities from the current 50 percent to 40 percent—a 20 percent reduction. MADD will urge the American public and all levels of government to adopt a similar goal, which can be achieved through the accomplishment of specific objectives in five major areas dealing with youth issues, enforcement, sanctions, self-sufficiency programs, and responsible marketing and service.

Youth Issues: Efforts to reduce youthful impaired driving and involvement in DWI offenses and crashes requires more than simply a minimum drinking age of 21. We must work to assure that alcohol-free areas are maintained, around schools and for regular functions; provide education to youth about the hazards of alcohol and other drugs; apply appropriate penalties to adults and older youths who supply alcohol and drugs to minors; and assess proper sanctions to youths who commit such offenses.

Enforcement: Enforcement of DWI laws requires the use of effective tools such as sobriety checkpoints, where and when allowed by law, modern technology such as preliminary breath tests and passive alcohol sensors, a *per se* limit set at an appropriate level such as .08, mandatory BAC testing when crashes result in loss of lives or in serious injury, and limits on open containers in vehicles.

Sanctions: Appropriate sanctions serve as effective deterrents to DWI crimes, as well as proper responses to offenses committed. Sanctions proven effective in reducing repeat offenses include administrative license revocation and jail for repeat offenders. Additional approaches designed to reduce repeat offenses include license plate/vehicle confiscation; increasingly severe penalties for further offenses such as greater fines and fees, longer jail and extended license revocation periods, etc.; and elimination of charge reduction negotiations. Establishment of minimum-security facilities for incarceration of DWI offenders would better accommodate such offenders while providing education/treatment as needed. Offenses resulting in death or serious bodily injury, as well as leaving the scene of such a crash, should be made felonies and should warrant equal penalties. Further, improvement should be made in systems to track offenses from arrest to disposition by courts or driver license agencies, in order to more effectively identify and deal with multiple offenders and to better document the impaired driving problem and effective solutions on a state by state and national basis judicial proceedings and legislative research.

Self-Sufficiency Programs: In order to ensure consistent, long-term funding for comprehensive impaired driving law enforcement, MADD advocates the channeling of DWI fines, fees and other assessments, including such user fees as alcohol excise taxes, into such programs.

Responsible Marketing Service: In keeping with MADD's non-prohibitionist stance of long standing, MADD advocates increased responsibility in both the marketing and serving of alcoholic beverages. While not calling for legislated limits on beverage advertising, MADD strongly urges that the industries involved monitor their efforts to avoid any depictions of dangerous or illegal use of alcohol, including special appeal to those under the legal purchase age. Any beverage promotions which encourage excessive consumption, such as "happy hours" multiple drink sales, should be ended. "Designated Driver" and other programs which reinforce a responsible approach to consumption should be encouraged. Further, the implementation of management and server training programs should be encouraged, and victims should be assured the right to seek financial recovery from establishments which irresponsibly provide alcohol to minors or intoxicated persons or who serve past the point of intoxication individuals who then cause fatal or injurious traffic crashes. Additional measures to reduce the likelihood of impaired driving include setting bar closing hours at a uniform time within a state and ultimately between states.

MADD's Victim Services

Each of the more than 23,000 fatalities and half a million serious injuries incurred yearly is a unique and irreplaceable individual with a name, a family, and dreams which must now go unfulfilled. Each represents far more than a faceless number to his or her family and friends, who are now caught in the tragic ripple effect set off by each crash.

For drunk driving victims — both injured persons and survivors of fatalities — MADD offers the following special services:

Crisis Intervention

Alcohol and other drug-related crashes create a critical period in the lives of victims. MADD victim advocates provide emotional support to help victims cope with their grief and anger. In addition, victims receive printed materials to help them understand the grieving process and guide them through the criminal justice system.

Victim Support

MADD brings victims together in victim support groups to discuss their feelings and futures. Victims offer each other a unique understanding and reassurance.

Victim Advocacy

Victims are offered a thorough explanation of the judicial process. MADD advocates clarify the victims' rights, accompany them to court when necessary and follow up on the sentencing of the offender. MADD offers the *Victim Information Pamphlet* to inform victims about their rights in court proceedings and *Financial Recovery After A Drunk Driving Crash* to inform them about victim compensation, insurance and civil suits. The *MADDVOCATE* provides up-to-date information for victims and victim advocates.

Victim Impact Panels (VIPs)

Judges or probation officers order convicted drunk drivers to attend a Victim Impact Panel as a component of their sentencing. The panel is composed of three or four victims of drunk driving crashes who tell their stories simply and from the heart. The goal of the program is to enable the offenders to understand their crime from the victim perspective and choose to never again drink and drive.

Information and Referral

MADD chapters refer victims to other agencies which offer financial and legal information, as well as professional counseling, as requested.

MADD and You

Grass roots activism is the force of MADD. Your unyielding determination, commitment, energy, courage and creativity, along with thousands of others, is needed to reduce the number of deaths and injuries from alcohol and other drug-related driving.

You can help us create a future that is less violent for everyone. We invite you to become actively involved in the work to end alcohol and other drug-impaired driving. Together we can make a difference because we are in it for lives.

There are various ways to participate actively in this bold cause:

- Be responsible for your own thinking and actions about drunk driving—*don't drink and drive.*
- Encourage your family and friends in being responsible for their thinking and actions about drunk driving—*friends don't let friends drive drunk.*
- Be informed about the issues of drunk driving. Make yourself knowledgeable so that you can create conversations with others that raise their consciousness and support them in being responsible. MADD provides numerous written materials to educate you, and we are just a telephone call away.
- Be actively involved at whatever level you can give. If your community has a MADD chapter, make your talent and time available to help. Explore the possibility of organizing a chapter in your community, if one does not exsist. If you prefer, work with other resources in your community to fight alcohol and other drug-related driving, or create resources that are missing.

Thank you! Through your financial contribution, you have expressed a commitment to end alcohol and other drug-related driving. We hope you will take the next step and become actively involved. Contact MADD in your local community or the National Office.

MADD National Office
669 Airport Freeway, Suite 310
Hurst, Texas 76053
817/268-6233

Mothers Against Drunk Driving

Soups, Stews and Casseroles

FOOD WRITERS'
FAVORITES

Contents

1 Information about MADD

12 Introduction

13 Freezing Tips

14 Contributing Editors

15 Poultry

31 Beef

51 Other Meats

65 Seafood

87 Cheese and Eggs

97 Rice and Noodles

111 Beans and Legumes

119 Vegetables

INTRODUCTION

"What's for dinner tonight?" It's an age-old question.

Whether you want a quick meal or an international adventure, *Soups, Stews and Casseroles* can provide the answer.

Soups, stews and casseroles are appropriate for many occasions. Most can be prepared quickly. Many are nutritious because the cook regulates the kind and amount of ingredients used. And all are simply good eating.

You can count on the recipes in this book to be good because they are the special favorites of food writers across the country. The book combines not only the tried-and-true personal favorites of food writers, but also many regional specialties.

For the purpose of this book, casseroles were very loosely defined as one-pot dishes. The line between soups and stews was somewhat blurred, too. Regardless of category, the recipes are sure to please.

In tune with today's lifestyles, the writers contributed more vegetable, poultry and seafood recipes than any other categories. You will, however, find that today's cooks rely on many convenience foods, and they are quick to use any ingredient that simplifies a recipe.

Each of the recipes in the book includes a brief introduction that tells you something about the recipe, so even if you aren't in the mood for cooking, the book makes for enjoyable reading.

We would like to make it clear that these recipes are the contributors' favorites. The publisher makes no claim that the recipes are original. When possible, credit has been given where credit is due. But in many cases, the recipes just evolved or have been handed down through families, and it is difficult, if not impossible, to say from where they came.

FREEZING TIPS

One reason why food writers enjoy making soups, stews and casseroles is because such dishes usually freeze well, so the effort involved in making a single recipe can yield two or more meals.

When freezing soups, stews and casseroles, keep these tips in mind:

* Follow the recipe, but, if possible, undercook the vegetables.

* Cool cooked dishes thoroughly before freezing.

* Leave ample head space to allow for the expansion of the liquid during freezing. Generally allow 1/2-inch for one-pint containers and 1-inch for 1-quart containers. Cubical containers allow for the most efficient use of freezer space.

* Label and date the packages. It is best to use frozen foods within one month for optimum flavor and texture.

* Do not freeze too much food at one time, because overloading the freezer raises the temperature to the detriment of already stored frozen foods.

* Always thaw frozen foods in their original containers, and it's best to thaw them in the refrigerator. Use all frozen items immediately after thawing because growth of bacteria can occur rapidly in thawed foods, especially casseroles.

* Most casseroles can be reheated in the oven from their frozen state. A general rule of thumb is to bake the casserole in a 350-degree oven until the mixture is hot throughout.

* Sometimes it is convenient to line baking dishes with foil, then fill them and freeze. When the foil-wrapped food is frozen solid, remove it from the dish, seal tightly and return immediately to the freezer. This allows you to use the baking dish until you are ready to reheat the food. When ready, remove the foil, return the frozen food to the baking dish and heat in the oven.

* If you plan to freeze a recipe from this or any cookbook, watch the seasonings carefully. Onion, pepper, celery, garlic and synthetic flavors tend to become strong or bitter; salt and herb flavorings decrease in strength; and curry acquires a musty flavor.

* To serve frozen soups, bring them to a boil in a saucepan, unless they are thick or have a cream base, in which case, a double boiler is necessary. For cold soups, thaw until liquid and serve chilled.

Whether you freeze these dishes or serve them immediately, the contributing writers hope you will enjoy this recipe collection. Happy cooking!

Contributing Food Editors

Barbara Mihalevich Arciero, *The Times,* Shreveport, LA
Betty W. Bernard, *Lake Charles American Press,* Lake Charles, LA
Barbara Bloch, *International Cookbook Services,* White Plains, NY
Beverly Bundy, *Fort Worth Star-Telegraph,* Fort Worth, TX
Barbara Burklo, *Santa Cruz Sentinel,* Santa Cruz, CA
Toni Burks, *Roanoke Times & World-News*, Roanoke, VA
Anne Byrn, *Atlanta Journal-Constitution*, Atlanta, GA
Sally Cappon, *Santa Barbara News-Press,* Santa Barbara, CA
Leona Carlson, *Rockford Register Star,* Rockford, IL
Sara Anne Corrigan, *The Evansville Press,* Evansville, IN
Beth Whitley Duke, *Amarillo Globe-News,* Amarillo, TX
Carolyn Flournoy, *The Times,* Shreveport, LA
June Ann Gladfelter, *The Express,* Easton, PA
Jane Witty Gould, *The Daily Journal,* Elizabeth, NJ
Patricia G. Gray, *The Express,* Easton, PA
Teri Grimes, *The Bradenton Herald,* Bradenton, FL
Paul Grondahl, *Albany Times Union*, Albany, NY
Lorrie Guttman, *Tallahassee Democrat,* Tallahassee, FL
Jim Hillibish, *The Repository,* Canton, OH
Monetta L. Horr, *Jackson Citizen Patriot,* Jackson, MI
Judy Johnson, *Mississippi Press,* Pascagoula, MS
Lori Longbotham, *New York Post,* New York City, NY
Miriam Morgan, *San Mateo Times,* San Mateo, CA
Adelaide A. Patten, *The Press of Atlantic City,* Pleasantville, NJ
Christine Randall, *Post-Courier Newspapers,* Charleston, SC
Florence D. Roggenbach, *Norfolk Daily News,* Norfolk, NE
Norma Schonwetter, *Micro Magic,* Oak Park, MI
Mary Denise Scourtes, *The Tampa Tribune,* Tampa, FL
Mattie Smith-Colin, *Chicago Defender*, Chicago, IL
Janet Geissler Watson, *Lansing State Journal,* Lansing, MI
Ann C. Wells, *The Grand Rapids Press,* Grand Rapids, MI

Poultry

16 Self-Crust Chicken Pie

17 Gourmet Chicken and Grits

18 Zesty Chicken and Dumplings

19 Baked Chicken with Orange-Nut Rice

20 New Mexican Enchilada Casserole

21 Turkey Tetrazzini

22 Turkey Sloppy Joes

23 Working Mom's Stew

24 South American Chicken

25 Super Summer Chicken

26 Turkey Chili

27 Chicken Breasts with Tomatoes and Shiitake Mushrooms

28 Chicken, Sausage and Rice Casserole

29 Chicken Casserole

30 Jenny's Chicken Pie

Self-Crust Chicken Pie

Anne Byrn
Food Editor, *Atlanta Journal-Constitution*, Atlanta, Georgia

No truly Southern recipe file could be complete without a good recipe for chicken pie. That's the sort of comfort food we Southerners grew up on and want to pass on to future generations. This version is a bit simpler than grandmother made, but it fits into modern lifestyles. The crust is a drop crust, requiring no rolling. Vegetables, such as onions and celery, can be added, if desired.

Makes 6 servings

- 2 cups chopped, cooked chicken or turkey
- 2 hard-cooked eggs, peeled and sliced
- 1-1/4 cups chicken or turkey broth
- 1 can (10-3/4 ounces) condensed cream of celery soup, undiluted
- 1/4 cup butter or margarine, softened
- 1 cup self-rising flour (see note)
- 1 cup milk
- 1/4 teaspoon black pepper

Place chicken in a 13x9x2-inch baking dish. Layer egg slices on top of chicken. In a medium saucepan, combine broth and celery soup; bring to a boil. Pour hot broth mixture over chicken and eggs.

In a medium mixing bowl, cut butter into flour; blend in milk and pepper. Spoon dough over mixture in baking dish. (Dough will not be smooth.)

Bake in a preheated 425-degree oven for 30 minutes, or until crust is browned.

Note: To make your own self-rising flour, add 1-1/2 teaspoons baking powder and 1/2 teaspoon salt to 1 cup all-purpose flour.

Gourmet Chicken and Grits

Lorrie Guttman
Food Editor, *Tallahassee Democrat*, Tallahassee, Florida

If you don't know what grits are, you're not from the South! Even Northerners can find grits in their grocery stores, near the cornmeal. This recipe is a good reason to give grits a try.

When grits are cooking, they tend to splatter, so put them in a deep saucepan, and stir them a little. This casserole is an unusual way to use leftover chicken or turkey. It came from one of our newspaper's recipe contests.

Makes 6 servings

- 2 cans (14-1/2 ounces each) chicken broth
- 1 cup quick (not instant) grits
- 3 eggs, beaten
- 1 jar (8 ounces) pasteurized process cheese spread, such as Cheez Whiz (use flavored version, if desired)
- 2 cups chopped, cooked chicken or turkey
- Generous pinch of curry powder
- Generous pinch of ground nutmeg
- 1/4 pound fresh mushrooms, sliced
- 2 tablespoons olive oil
- 1 can (10-3/4 ounces) condensed cream of mushroom soup, undiluted

In a large saucepan, bring broth to a boil; add grits. Cook about 5 minutes, stirring occasionally. Stir in beaten eggs, cheese spread, chicken, curry powder and nutmeg; mix well.

Transfer grits mixture to a greased 3-quart casserole. Bake, uncovered, in a preheated 375-degree oven for 30 minutes.

While grits are baking, saute mushroom slices in olive oil in a large skillet. Stir in mushroom soup. Continue cooking until mixture is hot.

Top each serving of grits with mushroom sauce.

Zesty Chicken and Dumplings

Toni Burks
Food Editor, *Roanoke Times & World-News*, Roanoke, Virginia

No one has ever made chicken and dumplings the way my Grandma did. Actually, it was the dumplings that were distinctive—flat strips of dough that cooked up tender but chewy, almost like fat noodles. Appreciation for Grandma's dumplings came too late to get her recipe, but after many years, I learned that Grandma had made what Eastern Shore folks call "slick dumplings." This updated version of Grandma's stew has a Southwestern accent, because the slick dumplings are made from flour tortillas.

Makes 4 servings

2 whole chicken breasts
1-1/2 quarts water
1/2 teaspoon salt
3 tablespoons butter or margarine
1 medium onion, finely chopped
2 cloves garlic, minced
1/2 to 1 teaspoon ground cumin, to taste
1/4 cup all-purpose flour
1 can (4 ounces) diced green chilies, undrained
1/2 cup half-and-half or light cream
Salt and black pepper, to taste
4 (8-inch) flour tortillas
Grated sharp Cheddar cheese

Rinse chicken and pat dry with paper towels. Put chicken in a 3-quart saucepan; add water and salt. Cover and simmer 45 minutes to 1 hour, or until chicken is tender. Remove chicken from broth and set aside to cool. Strain broth and reserve. When chicken is cool enough to handle, remove and discard skin and bones. Cut chicken into chunks and set aside.

Melt butter in a 3-quart saucepan. Add onion, garlic and cumin; cook, stirring, until onion is tender. Stir in flour. Gradually add 3 cups of reserved broth (if necessary, use water to complete measure). Cook and stir until thickened and smooth. Add green chilies. Stir in half-and-half. Season with salt and pepper to taste. Add reserved chicken. Bring mixture to a simmer.

Cut tortillas into 2x1-inch strips and drop into simmering chicken mixture. Cover and turn off heat. Let stand, covered, 15 minutes. Garnish each serving with grated Cheddar cheese.

Baked Chicken with Orange-Nut Rice

Toni Burks
Food Editor, *Roanoke Times & World News*, Roanoke, Virginia

Elegant, easy, economical—it's a winning combination for entertaining in today's busy world. The elegance of this dish comes from the flavorful teaming of ingredients. It's easy because once it's assembled and in the oven, there's no stirring or tending. And few meats are more economical than chicken. Chicken breasts are specified, but dark-meat parts can be used with equally delicious results.

Makes 4 servings

- 2 whole chicken breasts, cut into halves
- 1/3 cup all-purpose flour
- 2 teaspoons salt, divided
- 1/4 teaspoon ground white pepper
- 1/3 cup vegetable oil
- 1 cup water
- 1/2 cup orange juice
- 1 tablespoon grated orange rind
- 1/2 cup minced onion
- 1/4 cup butter, cut into pieces
- 2 tablespoons chopped pecans
- 2 tablespoons chopped pimento
- 1 tablespoon lemon juice
- 1-1/2 cups instant rice, uncooked

Rinse chicken and pat dry with paper towels. Combine flour, 1 teaspoon salt and pepper. Coat chicken pieces on all sides with flour mixture. Heat oil in a large skillet over medium heat. Add chicken pieces and brown on all sides.

In an 8x8x2-inch baking dish, combine water, orange juice, orange rind, onion, butter, pecans, pimento and lemon juice. Add rice and remaining 1 teaspoon salt. Stir to mix well. Place chicken pieces, skin-side up, in a single layer over rice mixture.

Cover pan with foil. Bake in a preheated 350-degree oven for 35 minutes. Uncover and continue to bake for 15 minutes, or until fork can be inserted in chicken with ease.

New Mexican Enchilada Casserole

Sally Cappon
Food Columnist, *Santa Barbara News-Press*, Santa Barbara, California

I originally received this recipe from a neighbor in Roswell, New Mexico, in 1964. At that time, Mexican food was not nearly as popular throughout the United States as it is today. The original recipe called for stewing a whole chicken and cutting it up. As I got busier and this became a family favorite and a big hit at pot lucks, I began substituting canned chicken, instant minced onion and pre-shredded cheese. As I open six cans and prepare this dish in five minutes, I feel shamelessly decadent!

Makes 6 to 8 servings

4 cans (5 ounces each) boned chicken
1 can (10 ounces) enchilada sauce
1 can (10-3/4 ounces) condensed cream of mushroom soup, undiluted
2 tablespoons instant minced onion
1/2 teaspoon garlic salt
1 package (10-1/2 ounces) corn chips, divided
1-1/2 cups shredded sharp Cheddar cheese
2 chicken bouillon cubes
1 cup boiling water
Parsley flakes
Paprika

In a large mixing bowl, combine chicken, enchilada sauce, mushroom soup, onion and garlic salt. Line a greased 12x8x2-inch baking dish with about two-thirds of the corn chips. Pour chicken mixture over chips. Sprinkle with cheese and cover with remaining corn chips.

In a small saucepan, combine bouillon cubes and boiling water; stir until dissolved. Pour over mixture in baking dish. Sprinkle with parsley flakes and paprika. Bake in a preheated 350-degree oven for 30 minutes, or until done.

Note: This casserole can be assembled a day ahead and refrigerated. Pour hot chicken broth over casserole just before it goes into the oven to bake.

Turkey Tetrazzini

Barbara Bloch
President, *International Cookbook Services*, White Plains, New York

I deliberately cook a bigger turkey at Thanksgiving than we need for dinner because we love cold turkey sandwiches and I like to serve Turkey Tetrazzini to company. When I don't want to make the casserole right away, I dice the cooked turkey and freeze it until I need it.

Makes 10 to 12 servings

3/4 cup butter or margarine, divided
1-1/2 pounds fresh mushrooms, thinly sliced
1/2 cup all-purpose flour
5 cups chicken stock or broth
1 cup light cream or milk
2 egg yolks
2 cups grated Parmesan cheese, divided
Salt and freshly ground pepper, to taste
6 cups diced, cooked turkey
1 package (16 ounces) thin spaghetti, cooked according to package directions and drained

Melt 1/4 cup butter in a large skillet. Add mushrooms; saute until browned. Set aside.

Melt remaining 1/2 cup butter in a large saucepan. Add flour and cook 2 minutes, stirring constantly. Slowly stir in chicken stock and light cream. Cook over low heat, stirring, until sauce begins to thicken. Remove from heat. Beat egg yolks in a small bowl; add 4 tablespoons of the sauce to egg yolks very slowly, beating constantly. Pour egg yolk mixture back into sauce and add 1 cup Parmesan cheese. Cook over low heat, stirring, just until cheese is melted. Season with salt and pepper.

Measure 1-1/2 cups sauce and set aside. Add reserved mushrooms, turkey and spaghetti to sauce remaining in saucepan. Stir gently until well mixed. Spoon mixture into a large casserole. Pour reserved 1-1/2 cups sauce over top. Sprinkle with remaining 1 cup Parmesan cheese.

Bake, uncovered, in a preheated 375-degree oven about 20 minutes, or until hot and bubbly. Briefly place under broiler to brown top.

Turkey Sloppy Joes

Lori Longbotham
Food Editor, *New York Post*, New York City, New York

Sloppy Joes are traditionally made with ground beef. This one-dish meal uses ground turkey and has lots of added vegetables. When you're ready to serve it, add the optional cole slaw for an even more wholesome and tastier Sloppy Joe. Serve it on a toasted crusty roll and you have a great meal that doesn't even need a salad.

Makes 4 servings

4 tablespoons vegetable oil, divided
2 medium onions, peeled and diced
2 red or green bell peppers, seeded and diced
3 cloves garlic, peeled and minced
1 rib celery, diced
1 carrot, peeled and grated
1 medium zucchini, grated
1/4 teaspoon ground cumin
1/4 teaspoon dried thyme
Cayenne pepper, to taste
1 pound raw ground turkey
1 bottle (12 ounces) chili sauce
1 can (14-1/2 ounces) chicken broth
2 tablespoons Worcestershire sauce
1 bay leaf
Salt, to taste
4 large seeded rolls, split and toasted
Cole Slaw (optional; recipe follows)

Heat 2 tablespoons oil in a large skillet over medium heat. Add onions, bell peppers and garlic; cook, stirring occasionally, about 8 minutes, or until vegetables are soft. Add celery, carrot, zucchini, cumin, thyme and cayenne pepper; cook 2 minutes. Remove vegetables from skillet; set aside.

Heat remaining 2 tablespoons oil in the same skillet. Stir in ground turkey. Cook, stirring and breaking up turkey with a wooden spoon, for 3 to 4 minutes, or until lightly golden. Add reserved vegetable mixture, chili sauce, chicken broth, Worcestershire sauce and bay leaf. Reduce heat and simmer, partly covered, stirring occasionally, about 15 minutes, or until sauce thickens slightly. Taste and adjust seasoning, adding salt and cayenne, if necessary. Remove and discard bay leaf.

Spoon hot turkey mixture onto bottoms of toasted rolls. Top with cole slaw, if desired, then add tops of rolls.

Cole Slaw

1-3/4 cups diced white cabbage
1 carrot, peeled and diced
1 green onion, minced
2 tablespoons vegetable oil
1 tablespoon cider vinegar
1 teaspoon granulated sugar

In a large mixing bowl, combine cabbage, carrot and green onion with oil, vinegar and sugar. Stir to blend completely. Serve with Turkey Sloppy Joes, if desired.

Working Mom's Stew

Mary Denise Scourtes
Food Writer, *Tampa Tribune*, Tampa, Florida

It doesn't matter how many recipes for chicken you have, there's always need for a few more. Working Mom's Stew is a good family dish because it's short on work and long on compliments. It's also great for buffet suppers. I like to serve it with white rice studded with almonds or saffron-scented rice.

Makes 4 servings

2 tablespoons vegetable oil
1 frying chicken (3 pounds), cut up
1 clove garlic, peeled and minced
1 onion, peeled and chopped
1 green bell pepper, seeded and chopped
1 can (2-1/2 ounces) sliced mushrooms, drained
3/4 teaspoon dried oregano
1 can (16 ounces) tomatoes, undrained
1/3 cup chicken broth or water
1/2 cup pitted ripe olives
4 anchovies, chopped (optional)

Heat oil in a large pot over medium-high heat. Add chicken, a portion at a time, without crowding. Cook, turning occasionally, until chicken is lightly browned on all sides. (Remove white pieces first because they cook the fastest.) Set chicken aside.

Discard all but a tiny bit of pan drippings. Add garlic, onion and bell pepper to pot; saute briefly. Add mushrooms, oregano, tomatoes with their liquid, chicken broth, olives and reserved chicken. Bring to a boil. Reduce heat and simmer for 30 minutes, turning chicken pieces once. Add anchovies, if using. Cook 10 minutes longer, or until chicken is tender.

South American Chicken

Norma Schonwetter
Syndicated Columnist, *Micro Magic*, Oak Park, Michigan

Canned tomato soup provides an easy shortcut to the South American flavor of this one-dish meal. A carrot-potato pudding is created as a result of the cooking process. A friend of mine, who prepares chicken every Friday, gave me the conventional recipe because her family liked it so well. I adapted it for the microwave oven. This recipe freezes well.

Makes 4 servings

- 2 tablespoons vegetable oil (for conventional method only)
- 2 whole chicken breasts, halved, skinned and boned (about 1 pound)
- 1 medium onion, chopped
- 1 to 2 ribs celery, chopped
- 1 can (10-3/4 ounces) reduced-sodium tomato soup, undiluted
- 3/4 teaspoon ground nutmeg
- 2-1/2 cups shredded raw potatoes
- 1 cup shredded raw carrots
- 1/3 cup orange juice
- 1/2 teaspoon salt, or to taste
- 1/8 teaspoon freshly ground black pepper
- 1/4 teaspoon Kitchen Bouquet or browning sauce (for microwave method only)

Heat oil in a large skillet over medium heat. Add chicken pieces; cook until browned. Set aside.

Add onion and celery to skillet; cook over medium-high heat until onion is soft. Stir in soup and nutmeg. Bring to a boil. Remove and reserve 1/2 cup soup mixture.

To remaining soup mixture in skillet, add potatoes, carrots, orange juice, salt and pepper. Stir well. Turn into a greased 13x9x2-inch baking dish. Top with chicken. Spoon reserved 1/2 cup soup mixture over chicken.

Bake in a preheated 375-degree oven for 30 minutes, or until chicken is tender.

Microwave method: Combine onion and celery in a microwave-safe 12x8x2-inch baking dish. Microwave, uncovered, on High (100 percent) power for 3 minutes. Stir in soup and nutmeg; remove and reserve 1/2 cup soup mixture.

To remaining soup mixture in baking dish, add potatoes, carrots, orange juice, salt and pepper. Stir well. Cover with vented plastic wrap and microwave on High power for 12 minutes, or until vegetables are just tender, stirring twice during cooking.

Place chicken pieces on top of vegetables; brush chicken with Kitchen Bouquet. Spoon reserved 1/2 cup soup mixture over chicken. Cover and microwave on High power 10 minutes. Rotate dish. Microwave on Medium (50 percent) power 5 minutes. Let stand 5 minutes, covered.

Super Summer Chicken

Teri Grimes
Food Editor, *The Bradenton Herald*, Bradenton, Florida

After growing my own herbs this summer, I have become obsessed with ways to use fresh mint—it grows so fast! This one-pot meal combines chicken and fresh mint with two of my favorite ingredients — garlic and fresh asparagus. It couldn't be simpler to prepare and offers the weekday cook yet another way to present chicken to the family.

Makes 6 servings

2 chickens (2-1/2 to 3 pounds each), cut up
Salt and pepper, to taste
2 pounds fresh asparagus, cleaned and trimmed
1/2 cup fresh mint leaves
1 clove garlic
2 lemons, thinly sliced
4 tablespoons butter, cut into pieces

Remove skin from chicken, if desired. Arrange chicken pieces in a roasting pan or Dutch oven. Lightly season with salt and pepper. Arrange asparagus spears over chicken. Mince mint and garlic; sprinkle over chicken and asparagus. Arrange lemon slices over all. Dot with butter. Cover. Bake in a preheated 350-degree oven for 30 to 45 minutes, or until chicken is cooked through.

Turkey Chili

Beverly Bundy
Food Writer, *Fort Worth Star-Telegram*, Fort Worth, Texas

Texans live and die by their chili. But even Texans, the most independent of souls, are starting to eat more nutritiously. Yankees can add beans to this chili — a true Texan never would!

Makes 10 servings

1/4 cup olive oil
3 pounds raw ground turkey
Water
6 tablespoons chili powder
3 teaspoons salt, or to taste
10 cloves garlic, peeled and minced
1-1/2 teaspoons ground cumin
1 teaspoon ground marjoram
1 teaspoon ground red pepper
1/2 teaspoon ground black pepper
1 tablespoon granulated sugar
1 tablespoon unsweetened cocoa powder
3 tablespoons ground paprika
4 tablespoons all-purpose flour
7 tablespoons cornmeal
Cooked pinto or kidney beans (optional)

Heat olive oil in a 6-quart pot. Add ground turkey; sear over high heat. Stir until meat is gray, not brown. Add 1 quart water. Bring to a boil and simmer for 1 hour; skim off fat. Add chili powder, salt, garlic, cumin, marjoram, red pepper, black pepper, sugar, cocoa powder and paprika. Simmer 30 minutes.

In a small bowl, combine flour, cornmeal and 3/4 cup cold water. Stir into turkey mixture; stir for 5 minutes. Mixture will be very thick. Let cool and store in refrigerator.

To serve, add water to make chili of desired consistency. Reheat to simmering; serve hot.

(Cooked pinto or kidney beans can be added to chili, if desired.)

Chicken Breasts with Tomatoes and Shiitake Mushrooms

Jane Witty Gould

Food Editor, *The Daily Journal*, Elizabeth, New Jersey

Couscous, a Moroccan specialty, is now available in the pasta section of most supermarkets. This nutty mini-pasta that can be steamed in minutes makes a satisfying alternative to rice, as in this chicken dish. Black shiitake mushrooms, an Asian specialty which is now available in many neighborhood supermarkets, add another kind of exotic flavor.

Make 4 to 6 servings

Quick-mixing flour (such as Wondra), for dredging
Salt and black pepper, to taste
3 whole chicken breasts, halved, skinned and boned
5 tablespoons margarine or butter
1 pint shiitake mushrooms, cleaned, stemmed and sliced into strips
Juice of 1/4 fresh lemon
1 can (12 ounces) Italian-style stewed tomatoes, undrained
Cooked couscous (follow package directions for preparation)

Season flour with salt and pepper. Lightly dredge chicken pieces in seasoned flour.

Melt margarine in a 12-inch, stainless-steel skillet. Saute 3 chicken pieces at a time over low heat for 2 to 3 minutes on each side. Remove to a plate. Season with salt and pepper.

Saute mushrooms in margarine remaining in skillet. Squeeze a few drops of lemon juice over mushrooms and the rest over chicken.

Add tomatoes with their liquid to mushrooms in skillet; simmer 1 minute. Add chicken with any accumulated juices to tomato mixture. Spoon some of the tomato mixture over the chicken. Simmer, uncovered, over low heat 10 minutes. Serve over couscous.

Chicken, Sausage and Rice Casserole

Patricia G. Gray
News Assistant, *The Express*, Easton, Pennsylvania

About 12 years ago, I tried this recipe that was in an advertisement for a cookbook club. Because it made a large quantity, I tried it for a Christmas Eve buffet that my husband and I hold for our relatives each year. The casserole was such a hit that it has become a traditional part of the buffet. If I don't include it, several people ask for it. Even my sister-in-law, who does not like rice, eats this casserole.

Over the years, I have made many changes in the recipe. I now use skinned, boned chicken breasts cut into bite-size pieces, because it is easier to eat at a party than the whole chicken cut into serving pieces, which is what was in the original recipe. I also eliminated salt and cut down on oil to make the recipe more healthful. A red bell pepper was added to the green for a touch of holiday color for Christmas, although the recipe is delicious any time of year.

Leftovers taste great, but I don't know if the dish can be frozen because I have never had enough left to try freezing it.

Makes 6 to 8 servings as a main dish;
up to 20 servings as a buffet dish

- 3 slices bacon, cut into small pieces
- 2 cups finely chopped onion
- 3 cloves garlic, peeled and minced
- 1 green bell pepper, seeded and chopped
- 1 red bell pepper, seeded and chopped
- 3/4 pound sweet sausage, cut into 1/2-inch slices
- 3/4 pound hot (spicy) sausage, cut into 1/2-inch slices
- 4 to 5 cups unsalted chicken broth (homemade, preferably)
- Freshly ground black pepper, to taste
- 1 tablespoon capers
- 1 teaspoon whole saffron, crushed
- 4 whole chicken breasts, skinned, boned and cut into bite-size pieces
- 1 tablespoon paprika
- 2 tablespoons olive oil
- 2 cups rice, uncooked
- 1 package (10 ounces) frozen peas, thawed

In a large skillet, combine bacon, onion, garlic, red and green peppers and sweet and hot sausages. Cook until onions are soft.

Spoon mixture into a 5-quart casserole dish. Add 1/4 cup broth, black pepper, capers and saffron; mix well.

Sprinkle chicken pieces with paprika. Heat olive oil in skillet. Add chicken and cook until brown on all sides. Add to sausage mixture.

Rinse rice in a colander; add to sausage-chicken mixture. Add 4 cups chicken broth. Bake, covered, in a preheated 400-degree oven 35 to 40 minutes, stirring once during baking. If rice becomes dry, add some or all of the remaining 3/4 cup chicken broth. When rice is tender, reduce oven temperature to 300 degrees. Uncover casserole and stir in peas. Cook 10 minutes longer. Serve hot.

Chicken Casserole

Monetta L. Horr
Food Editor, *Jackson Citizen Patriot*, Jackson, Michigan

I'm always looking for ways to serve chicken and this recipe is a family favorite. The water chestnuts add crunch and the herb-flavored stuffing mix seasons it so well. It only takes a few minutes to mix everything together, layer it in a casserole dish and bake.

Makes 5 to 6 servings

3 cups cubed, cooked chicken
1 can (4 ounces) sliced mushrooms, drained
1 can (8 ounces) sliced water chestnuts, drained
1 can (10-3/4 ounces) condensed cream of mushroom soup, undiluted
1/2 cup milk
1/2 of an 8-ounce package fine, herb-flavored stuffing mix
1/2 cup water
1/4 cup margarine, melted

Grease a 12x9x3-inch loaf pan or 2-quart casserole dish.

In a large mixing bowl, combine chicken, mushrooms and water chestnuts; pour into bottom of pan. In a small bowl, combine soup and milk; pour over chicken mixture. In a medium mixing bowl, combine stuffing mix, water and margarine. Spoon over mixture in pan. Bake in a preheated 350-degree oven for 25 minutes.

Jenny's Chicken Pie

Carolyn Flournoy
Food Writer, *The Times*, Shreveport, Louisiana

This recipe was given to me by a friend in Beaumont, Texas, although in a slightly different form. I like to take it to families just back from vacation, or when someone is ill, or as a housewarming gift, or just "because." You can add pearl onions or sliced carrots or both, if you like. Sometimes I bake the casserole in two smaller dishes — one to eat and one to freeze.

Makes 10 to 12 servings

4 to 5 cups chopped, cooked chicken
1 can (10-3/4 ounces) condensed cream of mushroom soup, undiluted
1 can (10-3/4 ounces) condensed cream of chicken soup, undiluted
1/2 cup milk
1/2 cup dairy sour cream
1 jar (6 ounces) sliced mushrooms, drained
1 can (8 ounces) small English peas, drained
1-1/2 teaspoons lemon juice
1 teaspoon Worcestershire sauce
Salt and seasoned pepper, to taste

For crust:
1 cup buttermilk baking mix
1/3 cup cornmeal
3/4 cup milk
1 egg, slightly beaten
2 cups grated Cheddar cheese

In a large mixing bowl, combine chicken, mushroom soup, chicken soup, milk, sour cream, mushrooms, peas, lemon juice, Worcestershire sauce, salt and seasoned pepper. Pour into a greased 13x9x2-inch baking dish (or a 3-quart casserole dish).

For crust: In another mixing bowl, combine baking mix, cornmeal, milk, egg and cheese; mix well.

Using a spoon, drop dough onto chicken mixture in mounds. Bake in a preheated 350-degree oven for 30 minutes. The crust should be light to medium brown.

Beef

32 Lake Erie Clipper Soup
33 Southern Pot Roast
34 Cajun Stuffed Peppers
35 Great Pumpkin Meatloaf
36 Frontier Stew
37 Nutty Noodle Casserole
38 Swedish Meat Soup
39 Baked Steak
40 Brazilian Chuck Roast
41 Chili Con Carne
42 Moussaka
43 Borscht
44 Sweet-and-Sour Beef and Cabbage
45 Beef Sukiyaki
46 Kohlrabi Stew
47 Oven Stew
48 Uruguayan-Style Meat Pie
49 Stifado
50 Chile Relleno Casserole

Lake Erie Clipper Soup

Jim Hillibish
Food Editor, *The Repository*, Canton, Ohio

Northern Ohioans suffer winter blasts of Arctic air riding deep, fast-moving troughs of low pressure from Canada. These Alberta clippers, as we call them, blow in minus-20-degree wind chills and howling storms. Nights such as these require something strong, fortifying and satisfying. That means thick, rich soup, almost a stew, the kind that makes a meal in a bowl. Don't forget the crusty sourdough bread, heaped high with apple butter — maybe tomorrow will be better.

Makes 4 servings

- 5 cups beef broth, divided
- 1 teaspoon dried thyme
- 1 tablespoon olive oil
- 2 cloves garlic, peeled and minced
- 1 pound beef stew meat, cut into 1/2-inch cubes
- 2 medium onions, peeled and chopped
- 1 bay leaf
- 1/4 cup pearl barley, uncooked
- 1/2 cup small shell macaroni, uncooked
- 2 cups stewed tomatoes
- Salt and freshly ground black pepper, to taste

In a large saucepan, bring 4 cups broth to a simmer. Add thyme.

Heat olive oil in a heavy soup pot; add garlic. When you can smell the garlic in the steam, add stew meat and onion; brown. Drain fat.

Add hot beef broth to meat in soup pot. Stir, scraping up browned bits from bottom. Add bay leaf. Boil 5 minutes, skim the surface, then cover tightly and simmer gently for 1 hour. Add remaining 1 cup broth. Bring to a boil. Add pearl barley, macaroni and stewed tomatoes. Season with salt and pepper to taste. Simmer for 30 minutes, or until macaroni is tender.

Note: This soup freezes well.

Southern Pot Roast

Barbara Bloch
President, *International Cookbook Services,* White Plains, New York

I don't know if this is really a Southern recipe, but my husband, who was born and raised in Florida, has always called it Southern Pot Roast. This is the way his mother cooked it. It was clear to me, early in our marriage, that the key to a happy marriage for me would be to learn to cook pot roast this way. The meat should be cooked until it is very tender and, to be authentic, it must be served with hot, spicy, chow-chow pickles.

Makes 6 to 8 servings

1 boneless beef bottom or top round roast (3-1/2 to 4 pounds)
2 cups beef broth
1 can (15 ounces) stewed tomatoes, broken up, undrained
1 can (15 ounces) tomato sauce
1 large onion, peeled and chopped
1 green bell pepper, seeded and diced
1 clove garlic, peeled and minced
1 teaspoon granulated sugar (optional)
Salt and black pepper, to taste
6 to 8 potatoes, peeled and cut in half
6 to 8 carrots, peeled and cut into 2-inch chunks
16 small white onions
Salted water

Place meat in broiler pan. Brown on all sides under broiler; set aside.

Place broth, stewed tomatoes, tomato sauce, chopped onion, green pepper, garlic, sugar, salt and pepper in a large, heavy saucepot or Dutch oven; stir until ingredients are well mixed. Add meat; bring liquid to a boil, then reduce heat, cover, and cook 3 to 3-1/2 hours, or until meat is very tender. Turn meat over occasionally during cooking and add more liquid, if necessary.

While meat is cooking, cook potatoes, carrots and white onions in lightly salted water until just tender; drain and set aside.

Add cooked vegetables to meat during the last 15 minutes of cooking. Remove meat to carving board and slice. Taste sauce and adjust seasoning. Spoon sauce and vegetables into a large serving bowl. Serve meat with sauce spooned over it.

Cajun Stuffed Peppers

Carolyn Flournoy
Food Columnist, *The Times*, Shreveport, Louisiana

Meal clean-up can be much easier if the individual casserole dishes are edible — as in the case of stuffed peppers. This is one of my family's favorite recipes and is usually requested for birthday dinners. My version is patterned after the Cajun stuffed peppers served along the bayous, making a South Louisiana specialty of this old-time dish. Part of the secret is the use of herbs and two cheeses. I freeze these on a tray, then put them in a plastic bag and return to freezer, to be removed in amounts needed.

Makes 12 to 16 halves

6 to 8 medium green bell peppers
1 pound lean ground beef (chuck or round)
1 cup chopped onion
1/4 cup chopped celery with leaves
1 teaspoon minced garlic
1/2 teaspoon salt
1/2 teaspoon black pepper
1/2 teaspoon dried thyme
1/2 teaspoon dried basil
1/2 teaspoon hot pepper sauce
1 can (16 ounces) tomatoes, drained, reserving the liquid
2 cups cooked rice
1-1/2 tablespoons Worcestershire sauce
1-1/2 cups grated Cheddar cheese
1/3 cup grated Parmesan cheese

Cut peppers in half lengthwise; remove stems and seeds. Blanch peppers in boiling salted water for 3 to 4 minutes; remove peppers from water and drain in a colander.

In a skillet with a heavy bottom, brown ground beef for a few minutes, stirring occasionally; add onions and celery. Cook, stirring for 3 to 4 minutes. Drain off fat.

Add garlic, salt, pepper, thyme, basil and hot pepper sauce; stir and cook 1 minute. Add drained tomatoes, stirring to break them up; cook 5 minutes. Add cooked rice and Worcestershire sauce; stir to mix. Cover and simmer over low heat 10 minutes, adding some of the reserved tomato liquid as necessary. Remove from heat. Stir in cheeses.

Stuff pepper halves with meat mixture. Place in a pan with a little water in the bottom. Bake, uncovered, in a preheated 350-degree oven for 25 to 30 minutes.

Note: Stuffed peppers and excess stuffing can be frozen.

Great Pumpkin Meatloaf

Beverly Bundy

Food Writer, *Fort Worth Star-Telegram,* Fort Worth, Texas

This meat-stuffed pumpkin recipe won the Fort Worth Star-Telegram*'s cooking-with-pumpkin contest a few years ago. The dish is fun in its presentation and it's easy for the cook because the vegetable cooks with the meat. It's the perfect meal for a cool autumn evening.*

Makes 6 to 8 servings

1 small pumpkin (3-1/2 to 4 pounds)
Salt and black pepper, to taste
3 tablespoons prepared yellow mustard, divided
2 tablespoons brown sugar
1 egg
1 tablespoon Worcestershire sauce
1/2 teaspoon salt, or to taste
1-1/2 pounds lean ground beef
1/2 cup fine dry bread crumbs

Cut top from pumpkin; discard top. Remove and discard strings and seeds. Place whole pumpkin, minus top, in baking dish. Add about 1 inch hot water to dish around the outside of the pumpkin. Cover pumpkin and pan with foil. Bake in a preheated 400-degree oven for 45 minutes, or until pumpkin is tender but not falling apart. Pour off water.

Season inside of pumpkin with salt and pepper. Spread with 1 tablespoon mustard and sprinkle with brown sugar.

Combine remaining 2 tablespoons mustard, egg, Worcestershire sauce, salt, ground beef and bread crumbs. Mix well. Spoon beef mixture into pumpkin shell, packing down tightly.

Return pumpkin to 400-degree oven and bake, uncovered, for 45 minutes to 1 hour, or until pumpkin is tender and meatloaf is cooked. Cut into wedges to serve.

Frontier Stew

Beverly Bundy
Food Writer, *Fort Worth Star-Telegram,* Fort Worth, Texas

Beef is king in Texas. Adding vegetables brings this stew into the modern ages. Add corn bread, and you have a meal that no cowhand would brand as sissy.

Makes 6 to 8 servings

1-1/2 pounds ground beef
1 tablespoon bacon drippings
1 medium onion, peeled and chopped
1/4 cup green bell pepper, seeded and chopped
1 clove garlic, peeled and minced (or 1 teaspoon garlic powder)
1/4 cup chopped celery
1 tablespoon chili powder
1/4 teaspoon granulated sugar
Salt and black pepper, to taste
1 can (16 ounces) whole tomatoes, undrained
1 can (16 ounces) whole-kernel corn, undrained
1 can (32 ounces) Ranch-Style beans, undrained (see note)
6 medium potatoes, peeled and cubed
3 cups water

Brown ground beef in bacon drippings, separating meat with a fork as it cooks. Add onion, green pepper, garlic and celery; cook until vegetables are soft. Add chili powder, sugar, salt and pepper; mix well. Add tomatoes with their liquid, breaking them up with a knife or the back of a spoon. Add corn, beans, potatoes and water. Bring to a boil, stirring well.

Reduce heat. Cover and simmer until potatoes are tender. Stir occasionally during cooking.

Note: Ranch-Style beans are spicy pinto beans that are produced in Fort Worth. They are available in many supermarkets across the country. If not available, use any brand of canned pinto beans, and, if desired, add chopped green chilies.

Nutty Noodle Casserole

Ann C. Wells
Food Editor, *The Grand Rapids Press*, Grand Rapids, Michigan

A bachelor friend, Mick Searl of Grand Rapids, who loved to entertain but didn't like to cook, prided himself on being able to make this casserole. No matter how many times he served it, the guests didn't mind — it is so tasty!

For years he was unwilling to part with the recipe, but about 10 years ago, he finally relented. Mick insists the dish must be made with ground sirloin, but I find lean ground chuck is just as good and certainly less expensive.

The recipe has become a favorite of ours for Friday night suppers at our summer home on Lake Michigan because it can be made in advance, serves a gang and can be kept hot as family members arrive at various times throughout the evening.

Makes 10 generous servings

- 2 pounds ground sirloin (or lean ground beef)
- 1 medium onion, peeled and chopped
- 1 package (12 ounces) narrow egg noodles, cooked according to package directions and drained
- 1 can (10-3/4 ounces) condensed cream of mushroom soup, undiluted
- 1/2 cup sliced, pimiento-stuffed green olives
- 1/2 pound sharp Cheddar cheese, grated
- 1 can (3 ounces) chow mein noodles
- 1 can (6-1/2 ounces) mixed nuts

In a large skillet, brown ground beef with onion. Drain off any excess fat. Add cooked egg noodles, mushroom soup, olives and cheese; mix well. Turn into a 2-1/2- or 3-quart casserole dish.

Cover and bake in a preheated 350-degree oven for 30 minutes. Uncover; top with chow mein noodles and nuts. Return to oven and bake, uncovered, for 30 minutes.

Note: The baked casserole freezes well.

Swedish Meat Soup

Adelaide A. Patten
Food Writer, *The Press of Atlantic City*, Pleasantville, New Jersey

The Swedish people are well known for their love of vegetables and soups. This recipe is my version of Koettsoppa, a beef and vegetable soup that has no added thickeners.

Chewy, whole-grain breads are a natural accompaniment to this fragrant soup that makes a substantial luncheon or dinner dish. Add some fruit and Swedish cheese to your menu and you have a robust meal.

Makes 8 to 10 servings

1 to 1-1/2 pounds beef bones
2 to 2-1/2 pounds beef (shin, plate or chuck)
2-1/2 quarts cold water
1-1/2 teaspoons salt, or to taste
1 medium onion, peeled
4 whole cloves
6 green onions or 1 leek, cut into 1/2-inch slices
3 ribs celery, diced
1 white turnip, peeled and diced
3 large carrots, peeled and diced
1/2 teaspoon ground white pepper, or to taste

Put the beef bones, beef and cold water into a large soup pot. Cover and cook over high heat until water boils. Add salt and onion studded with cloves. Reduce heat to simmer; cook for 2 to 2-1/2 hours, or until meat is tender, skimming frequently.

Carefully remove bones, meat and onion from broth. Discard bones and clove-studded onion. (If using marrow bones, push out the marrow and add it to the broth.)

Cover meat to keep it from drying out and set aside.

Increase heat under soup pot and return broth to boiling. Add green onions, celery, turnip and carrots. Cover; bring to boil again. Reduce heat and simmer vegetables for 1 hour. Taste; add white pepper and, if necessary, more salt.

Cut meat into bite-size pieces and add to soup. Simmer 5 minutes.

Ladle soup into heated soup dishes. Serve with thinly sliced, whole-grain, European-style bread and unsalted butter.

Baked Steak

Jane Witty Gould
Food Editor, *The Daily Journal,* Elizabeth, New Jersey

Baked steak was a childhood favorite that my mother served in the winter when we had a craving for steak but when it was too cold to barbecue.

Many years later, I was stunned to make its acquaintance, albeit in a more sophisticated form, as "steak au four" on Julia Child's television show. America's favorite television chef showed a shoulder steak slathered with butter and surrounded by garlic. But underneath that Gallic peppercorn crust beat the heart of a true American, my old friend, baked steak, straight out of my mother's '50s "Settlement Cookbook." With a little tinkering it has become my own children's childhood favorite.

Makes 4 servings

1 top sirloin or top round boneless beef steak (about 3 pounds), trimmed of all fat, 1-1/2 inches thick
2 teaspoons olive oil
Salt and freshly ground black pepper, to taste
1 small green bell pepper, seeded and cut into 1/8-inch rings
1 small onion, peeled and cut into 1/8-inch rings
3 cloves garlic, peeled and minced
1 can (14 ounces) Italian-style stewed tomatoes, drained
1/2 cup ketchup

Dry steak with paper towels. Spread oil on both sides of steak, making a light film. Brown steak in a ridged cast-iron skillet 2 minutes. Turn steak a quarter-turn without turning over; brown another 2 minutes to make cross marks. Repeat on other side; 8 minutes cooking time in all.

Transfer steak to oven-proof dish or skillet, just large enough for steak to fit comfortably with the vegetables. Season with salt and pepper. Pile green pepper and onion rings on top of steak. Sprinkle with garlic. Top with stewed tomatoes. Pour ketchup over all.

Bake in upper third of a preheated 400-degree oven for 40 minutes, for medium rare. (Test after 30 minutes with a meat thermometer.) Slice and serve each portion with some of the vegetables.

Note: If using a thinner steak, reduce cooking time.

Brazilian Chuck Roast

Norma Schonwetter
Syndicated Columnist, *Micro Magic*, Oak Park, Michigan

For years I had looked at this weird recipe that used coffee in the gravy for a chuck roast. Finally one day, I decided to try it as a microwave dish. I was delighted with the rich, dark flavor of the gravy that, surprisingly, was devoid of coffee taste. Everyone liked it, although I never told them that it had coffee in it, until after they tasted it.

Makes 8 servings

- 2 tablespoons vegetable oil (for conventional method)
- 1 boneless beef chuck roast (about 3 pounds), trimmed
- 1-1/2 cups strong coffee (1 cup for microwave method)
- 1 clove garlic, peeled and minced
- 1/2 teaspoon salt, or to taste
- 1/4 teaspoon ground black pepper
- 1/2 teaspoon dried leaf thyme
- 1 medium onion, peeled and cut into thick slices
- 4 small potatoes, unpeeled and cut into fourths
- 2 tablespoons all-purpose flour mixed with 1 tablespoon water

Heat oil in a heavy, 4-quart saucepot. Add chuck roast; brown on all sides. Add coffee, garlic, salt, pepper and thyme. Arrange onion slices on top of meat. Cook over high heat until boiling, stirring occasionally. Reduce heat to low and cook, covered, 1 hour. Add potatoes; continue to cook until meat and potatoes are tender. Remove meat and vegetables from pan juices; keep warm.

Blend flour with water to dissolve flour; stir into pan juices. Cook over medium-high heat until thickened, stirring constantly.

Slice meat and serve with pan gravy and vegetables.

Microwave method: Omit vegetable oil. Place meat in a 3-quart microwave-safe casserole dish. Combine 1 cup coffee, garlic, salt, pepper and thyme; pour over meat. Arrange onion slices on top of meat. Microwave, covered, on High (100 percent) power for 15 minutes, or until liquid is boiling; stir occasionally. Add potatoes; microwave, covered, on Medium (50 percent) power for 1 hour, or until meat and vegetables are tender. Remove meat and vegetables from pan juices; keep warm.

Blend flour with water to dissolve flour; stir into pan juices. Microwave, uncovered, 4 minutes on High power, or until thickened, stirring once.

Slice meat and serve with pan gravy and vegetables.

Chili Con Carne

Leona Carlson

Food Writer, *Rockford Register Star*, Rockford, Illinois

This chili recipe claims the distinction of being one of my rare successes in the first year of my marriage, when my culinary experience was largely limited to popcorn, fudge and, oddly enough, egg salad sandwiches. It's a mild, but good, chili. If you like your chili hot, just increase the amount of chili powder, but please—do it gingerly.

Makes 3 to 4 servings

1/2 cup chopped onion
1 clove garlic, peeled and minced
Vegetable oil (optional)
1 pound lean ground beef
2 cans (10-3/4 ounces each) condensed cream of tomato soup, undiluted
1 can (16 ounces) kidney beans, undrained
1 to 2 tablespoons chili powder
1/2 teaspoon salt, or to taste

Saute onion and garlic in a large, iron or other heavy skillet. Use a small amount of oil, if necessary. Add beef and saute until well done, stirring occasionally. Drain off all fat. Add soup, beans, chili powder and salt. Mix well. Cover and cook slowly for 1 hour, stirring periodically to prevent sticking. Use the lowest heat setting to maintain a simmer.

Note: This recipe can be doubled or tripled. It's best if eaten immediately; refrigerated leftovers have a tendency to dry out.

Moussaka

Norma Schonwetter
Syndicated Columnist, *Micro Magic*, Oak Park, Michigan

My favorite Greek dish is Moussaka. I prefer my version to the classic restaurant type because restaurants tend to use too much cinnamon and/or nutmeg. When I started growing eggplants in my garden, I found this was a great way to use them. I especially like this dish because I can make a double batch and freeze half; then thaw, cut into squares, and reheat in the microwave oven.

Makes 4 servings

- 2 medium eggplants
- Vegetable oil
- 1 pound lean ground beef
- 2 medium onions, peeled and chopped
- 2 cloves garlic, peeled and crushed
- 1 can (8 ounces) tomato sauce
- 1 teaspoon dried leaf oregano
- 1 teaspoon salt, divided
- 1/4 teaspoon black pepper, divided
- 2 tablespoons butter or margarine
- 2 tablespoons all-purpose flour
- 1 cup low-fat milk
- 1 egg
- 1/3 cup grated Parmesan cheese

Peel eggplants; slice 1/4-inch thick. Brush rimmed cookie sheet with oil. Coat each slice of eggplant on both sides with oil; place on cookie sheet. Broil close to broiler until brown. Turn; brush with oil, if necessary. Brown the other side. Repeat with all the eggplant slices.

Arrange half of the eggplant slices in the bottom of a lightly greased 9x9x2-inch baking dish.

In a large skillet, combine beef and onions. Cook, stirring constantly, until beef is brown and onions are soft. Drain off fat and juices. Add garlic, tomato sauce, oregano, 1/2 teaspoon salt and 1/8 teaspoon pepper. Pour over eggplant slices.

Arrange remaining eggplant slices over meat mixture.

Prepare cheese sauce: Melt margarine in a saucepan. Stir in flour, remaining 1/2 teaspoon salt and remaining 1/8 teaspoon pepper. Gradually stir in milk. Cook and stir over medium heat until thick and bubbly. In a small bowl, beat egg; stir in some of the hot sauce, then add egg to sauce mixture; mix well. Add cheese and stir again.

Pour cheese sauce over mixture in baking dish. Bake in a preheated 350-degree oven for 45 minutes. Cut into squares.

Note: When doubling recipe, triple the amount of sauce and use a 13x9x2-inch baking dish.

Borscht

Florence D. Roggenbach
Food Editor, *Norfolk Daily News*, Norfolk, Nebraska

My father taught his young wife how to cook, using recipes brought to this country by his family from Czechoslovakia. Many of these recipes were revised somewhat by my father, who loved to cook. He rarely missed making the entire Sunday dinner as well as holiday dinners. This is one of his specialties.

Makes 8 cups; 4 to 8 servings

3 cups hot water
1 pound beef, cut into cubes
3 medium beets, divided
2 medium carrots, peeled and sliced
1 medium onion, peeled and sliced
1 rib celery, cut into chunks
1 bay leaf
2-1/2 teaspoons salt, divided
1/2 of a 6-ounce can tomato paste
1-1/2 teaspoons granulated sugar
1 small head cabbage, shredded
1 tablespoon vinegar
1/2 cup dairy sour cream

In a large covered saucepot or Dutch oven over medium-low heat, combine hot water, beef, 2 sliced beets, carrots, onion, celery, bay leaf and 1-1/2 teaspoons salt; simmer for 2 hours.

Shred remaining 1 beet; add to mixture along with tomato paste, sugar and remaining 1 teaspoon salt. Simmer, covered, for 20 minutes. Remove and discard bay leaf. Refrigerate to blend flavors.

About 30 minutes before serving: Skim fat from soup. Over medium heat, bring soup to a boil. Add cabbage; cook about 15 minutes, or until cabbage is tender. Stir in vinegar. Serve garnished with sour cream.

Sweet-and-Sour Beef and Cabbage

Norma Schonwetter
Syndicated Columnist, *Micro Magic*, Oak Park, Michigan

A friend of mine originally made this recipe. She liked it because it tasted like stuffed cabbage rolls, but it was so easy to make. I adapted it for the microwave oven. I have made it with ground turkey as well as ground beef; either way is good. It's a complete meal when served with mashed potatoes.

Makes 4 servings

1 pound lean ground beef
1 medium onion, peeled and finely chopped
2 cloves garlic, peeled and minced
1 can (16 ounces) tomato sauce
1/4 cup applesauce
3 tablespoons apple cider vinegar
1 to 2 tablespoons dark brown sugar
1/4 teaspoon dried leaf thyme
Pinch of ground black pepper
4-1/2 cups finely shredded cabbage (about 1 pound)
1/4 cup raisins (optional)

In a Dutch oven or large saucepot over medium high heat, brown beef, breaking it with a spoon into small pieces. As it browns, add onion and garlic; continue to cook until meat is brown and onion is tender. Drain and discard fat.

Return pan to medium heat. Add tomato sauce, applesauce, vinegar, brown sugar, thyme and pepper to meat mixture in pan; mix well. Bring mixture to a boil, stirring constantly. Stir in cabbage and raisins. Reduce heat and simmer, covered, for 20 to 25 minutes, stirring occasionally, until cabbage is very tender. If sauce is too thin, uncover and cook for a few minutes to reduce the sauce.

Microwave method: Place meat, onion and garlic in a microwave-safe colander set in a 3-quart microwave-safe casserole dish. Microwave on High (100 percent) power 5 minutes, stirring once, until meat is no longer pink. Discard drippings. Transfer meat mixture to casserole dish. Stir in tomato sauce, applesauce, vinegar, brown sugar, thyme and pepper. Cover and microwave on High power for 5 minutes. Stir in cabbage and raisins. Microwave, covered, on High power 10 minutes; stir well. Microwave, covered, on Medium (50 percent) power until cabbage is crisp-tender. Let stand 10 minutes.

Beef Sukiyaki

Lori Longbotham
Food Editor, *New York Post*, New York City, New York

Here's a great Japanese one-dish meal that cooks in less than 20 minutes. This complete meal in a skillet has been adapted to American kitchens, and all the ingredients should be available in local supermarkets. It's prepared quickly and is a great way to begin cooking Japanese style.

Makes 4 servings

- 1/4 cup vegetable oil
- 1 medium onion, sliced thin
- 5 green onions, cut into 2-inch lengths
- 1 cup peeled, sliced daikon radish (optional)
- 1 cup finely shredded cabbage, preferably curly cabbage
- 1 pound boneless beef sirloin, sliced paper thin and cut into 3-inch pieces
- 10 fresh mushroom caps, sliced thin
- 1 cake (10 ounces) firm tofu, cut into 1-inch cubes
- 4 cups spinach leaves or shredded Swiss chard, washed well and drained
- 1 cup bean sprouts
- 1 cup canned beef broth
- 1/4 cup low-sodium soy sauce
- 2 tablespoons light brown sugar
- Hot cooked rice
- 1 tablespoon toasted sesame seeds

Heat oil over medium heat in a large heavy skillet with a lid. Add onion and green onions; stir-fry about 2 minutes. Add radish and cabbage; stir-fry for 3 minutes. Place a layer of beef slices on top of cabbage, then layer the mushrooms, tofu, spinach and bean sprouts.

In a small bowl, combine beef broth, soy sauce and brown sugar; stir until sugar is dissolved. Pour over layered mixture in skillet. Cook, covered, for 3 minutes on medium heat. Uncover and cook, stirring constantly, for 2 to 3 minutes.

Serve hot over cooked rice, garnished with sesame seeds.

Kohlrabi Stew

Jim Hillibish
Food Editor, *The Repository,* Canton, Ohio

Overheard in the produce department:

"I'm looking for some cold rabbi."

"Better try wines, Aisle 4, sir, perhaps between the Cold Duck and the Mogen David."

"Not wine, coal rubbi."

"In liniments I'm sure, sir, by the coal-tar dandruff shampoos perhaps...."

"No, it's a vegetable. Kohlrabi."

Once you get beyond its improbable German-Italian moniker, you'll find a vegetable that thinks it's a cabbage, but tastes closer to celery. It's very Old World German, but it is excellent as a substitute for potatoes in stews.

Makes 4 servings

- 1 cup plus 2 tablespoons unbleached flour, divided
- Freshly ground black pepper
- 1 teaspoon chili powder, or to taste
- 1 teaspoon salt, or to taste
- 1 pound beef stew meat, cut into bite-size pieces
- 5 carrots, peeled and sliced into rounds, divided
- 2 medium onions, peeled and thickly sliced
- 3 tablespoons bacon drippings or vegetable oil
- 4 cups beef broth, or more, if necessary
- 5 sprigs fresh parsley, chopped
- 2 bay leaves
- 4 kohlrabi
- Worcestershire sauce

In a large shallow pan, combine 1 cup flour, 1 teaspoon black pepper, chili powder and salt; mix well. Dust the meat, about 1/2 cup of the carrot rounds and the onion slices with flour mixture.

In a large stew pot or Dutch oven, heat bacon drippings. Saute beef and floured carrots and onions. When beef is brown, add beef broth, parsley and bay leaves. Season to taste with additional pepper, if desired. Cover tightly and simmer 2 hours. Check every 30 minutes and add more broth, if needed.

After stew has cooked 2 hours, peel kohlrabi and slice into 1/4-inch pieces. Add kohlrabi and remaining carrot rounds to stew. Simmer 45 minutes.

Make a thickener by combining the remaining 2 tablespoons flour with enough water to make a paste. Stir paste into simmering stew. When stew thickens, turn off heat and let stand, covered, for 10 minutes before serving. Serve with Worcestershire sauce.

Note: This freezes well. Kohlrabi, unlike potatoes, do not become grainy when frozen.

Oven Stew

Barbara Burklo

Retired Food Editor, *Santa Cruz Sentinel*, Santa Cruz, California

My mother, Flora Deemy, was an excellent cook. Above all, she paid attention to her cooking process and was fussy about every detail. At 94, she was still living alone and preparing her own meals with strict attention to proper nutrition. This was her favorite stew recipe. It makes a lovely gravy, without any fuss.

Makes 4 to 6 servings

1 can (15 ounces) tomatoes, undrained
3 tablespoons quick-cooking tapioca, uncooked
2 tablespoons dried basil
1 tablespoon granulated sugar
1 tablespoon salt, or to taste
Ground black pepper, to taste
1-1/2 pounds lean stew beef, cut into cubes
1 medium onion, peeled and chopped
2 to 3 carrots, peeled and cut into 1-inch lengths
2 to 3 potatoes, peeled and cut into 1-inch cubes
1 to 2 ribs celery, cut into 1-inch lengths

In a large Dutch oven, combine tomatoes with their liquid, tapioca, basil, sugar, salt and pepper. Add cubed beef, onion, carrots, potatoes and celery. Mix well.

Cover and bake in a 350-degree oven for 2 to 2-1/2 hours (see note), or until vegetables are tender and meat is well done. Stir occasionally.

Note: Burklo's mother's recipe called for baking the stew at 250 degrees for 5 hours; Burklo raised the temperature to 350 degrees. The stew can be cooked up to 5 hours, but 2 to 2-1/2 hours is adequate.

This stew freezes well.

Uruguayan-Style Meat Pie

Adelaide A. Patten
Food Writer, *The Press of Atlantic City*, Pleasantville, New Jersey

Having grown up in a "melting pot" neighborhood, I was exposed to various cuisines. Later I was delighted to get to know Americans who had spent several years in South America. One friend, who had lived in Uruguay, enjoyed making Pastel de Carne — Uruguayan Meat Pie. It was always a big hit at covered dish dinners. She had learned how to prepare this dish from the native woman who was her cook and housekeeper. Her method was a pinch of this and some of that. I diligently worked on a recipe that duplicated (almost) my friend's product. It contains ingredients with which you are familiar — nothing exotic.

Makes 4 generous servings

3/4 cup chopped onion
2 tablespoons unsalted butter
1-1/2 pounds well-trimmed round of beef, chopped
1 cup peeled, chopped tomatoes
Salt and freshly ground black pepper, to taste
3/4 cup raisins
1/2 cup unsalted butter, melted and cooled
1/2 cup milk
1/8 teaspoon salt
1/2 teaspoon white vinegar
1 to 1-1/2 cups all-purpose flour
1 egg, beaten
Parsley sprigs

For pie filling, saute onion over moderate heat in 2 tablespoons butter until limp and golden. Add beef, bit by bit, and cook until brown, breaking it up as much as possible during cooking.

Add tomatoes, salt, pepper and raisins. Cook gently for 10 minutes, stirring occasionally. Taste; adjust seasonings, if necessary. Set aside.

For crust, mix 1/2 cup melted butter with milk, 1/8 teaspoon salt and vinegar. Stir in enough flour to make a soft dough (the consistency of baking powder biscuit dough). Shape dough into a ball; divide in half.

Roll out one portion of dough until large enough to line a 9-inch pie pan. Fit dough loosely into pan. Roll out second portion of dough for pie top; set aside.

Spoon filling into dough-lined pan. Top with second portion of dough; seal edges and trim. Place pie on a baking sheet or jelly-roll pan. Brush top crust with beaten egg.

Bake in a preheated 400-degree oven 30 minutes, or until crust is a deep, golden brown. Do not overbake because a very brown crust will be bitter.

Cool pie on a wire rack for 5 to 10 minutes before serving. Garnish each serving with parsley sprigs.

Stifado

Mary Denise Scourtes
Food Writer, *The Tampa Tribune*, Tampa, Florida

The Greeks have a word for everything. Stifado is a robust dish that gets its flavor from the unusual combination of cinnamon and garlic. This recipe, often handed down among families for generations, is a Sunday mainstay in Greece and on the islands. (Both my paternal and maternal grandparents were born in Greece.)

It can be made with beef or lamb. The dish also freezes well.

Makes 6 servings

- 2 pounds stew beef, cubed (lamb can be substituted)
- 2 tablespoons olive oil
- 2 sticks cinnamon
- 2 cups beef broth, divided
- 4 small white onions, peeled and sliced
- 1 clove garlic, peeled and finely chopped
- 1 can (8 ounces) tomato sauce
- 1/2 teaspoon salt, or to taste

Trim meat of extra fat. Heat oil in a Dutch oven; brown meat. Add cinnamon sticks and 1 cup beef broth; cook 1-1/2 hours, or until meat is tender. Add onions and garlic; cook over low heat about 10 minutes. Add tomato sauce, remaining 1 cup beef broth and salt. Cook, covered, 30 minutes, or until meat is very tender. Remove and discard cinnamon sticks. Serve immediately.

Chile Relleno Casserole

Beth Whitley Duke

Food Editor, *Amarillo Globe-News*, Amarillo, Texas

Chiles Rellenos are a Tex-Mex specialty. Most recipes call for the chili pods to be scraped of their seeds, stuffed with cheese or meat and then dipped in batter and fried. This casserole version not only cuts down on preparation time, but also saves calories by bypassing the batter and hot oil.

Makes 6 servings

- 2 cans (4 ounces each) green chilies, drained, cut in halves crosswise and seeded
- 1 pound ground beef
- 1/2 cup chopped onion
- 1/2 teaspoon salt
- 1/4 teaspoon ground black pepper
- 1-1/2 cups grated Cheddar cheese
- 4 eggs, beaten
- 1-1/2 cups milk
- 1/4 cup all-purpose flour
- 1/3 cup picante sauce, or to taste

Spray a casserole dish with non-stick cooking spray. Arrange half of the chilies in the bottom of the dish.

Meanwhile, brown ground beef; drain fat. Simmer onions with beef; season with salt and pepper.

Top chilies with a layer of beef mixture, followed by a layer of cheese. Repeat layers of chilies, beef and cheese. Beat eggs with milk and flour. Gently pour egg mixture over casserole so as not to disturb layers.

Bake in a preheated 350-degree oven 45 to 50 minutes. Cut into squares to serve. Top with picante sauce, if desired.

Other Meats

52 Potato, Cheddar and Ham Casserole

53 Mid-Eastern Lamb-Stuffed Eggplant

54 East Indian Lamb Curry

55 Alligator Sauce Piquante

56 Tarragon Veal Stew

57 Liver Fricassee

58 Green Chili Pork

59 Sausage Dip

60 Chinese-Style Pork Chops with Three Mushrooms

61 Harvest Sweet Potato Meat Pie

62 Austrian-Style Ragout Soup with Bread Dumplings

64 Hurry-Up Pork Chops

Potato, Cheddar and Ham Casserole

June Ann Gladfelter
Assistant Managing Editor/Features, *The Express*, Easton, Pennsylvania

My mother, Minnie Gladfelter, developed this recipe over a number of years, first perfecting the potato-cheese combination, then adding the ham. It's a great one-dish meal that's been a family favorite for a long time. My sister takes leftovers to work for lunch and reheats them in a microwave oven.

The secret to preparing good scalloped potatoes, Mom says, is making a real white sauce. The dish is smoother and creamier when a white sauce, rather than just milk, is poured over the potatoes.

Makes 6 to 8 servings

- 6 medium potatoes, peeled and sliced
- 3 tablespoons butter or margarine
- 3 tablespoons all-purpose flour
- 1 teaspoon salt, or to taste
- 1/8 teaspoon ground black pepper
- 2 cups milk
- 1-1/2 cups grated Cheddar cheese
- 1 cup cubed, cooked ham
- 1 cup dry bread crumbs (optional)
- 2 tablespoons butter or margarine, melted (optional)

Put sliced potatoes in a saucepan; cover with water. Bring to a boil. Immediately remove from heat and drain. Transfer to a greased 2-quart baking dish or casserole dish.

While potatoes are coming to a boil, make a white sauce. Melt 3 tablespoons butter in a saucepan. Stir in flour, salt and pepper. Cook over low heat, stirring constantly, until mixture begins to bubble. Remove pan from heat and slowly add milk, stirring constantly. Return saucepan to heat and bring to a boil, stirring constantly. When white sauce is slightly thickened, add cheese. Continue stirring over medium heat until cheese is melted.

Pour cheese sauce over potatoes in baking dish. Add ham and mix gently, being careful not to break up potato slices.

If desired, combine bread crumbs and 2 tablespoons melted butter in a small bowl; sprinkle over casserole.

Bake in a preheated 350-degree oven for 1 hour, or until hot and bubbly.

Mid-Eastern Lamb-Stuffed Eggplant

Barbara Bloch
President, *International Cookbook Services,* White Plains, New York

The authentic version of this recipe uses ground lamb. However, if you don't happen to like lamb, you can substitute lean ground beef. You also can substitute feta or even Cheddar cheese for the mozzarella, if you like. And, if you want to serve this to company, you can double the recipe without making any changes in cooking time.

Makes 4 servings

- 2 medium eggplants (about 3/4 pound each)
- 1 pound lean ground lamb (or beef)
- 1 large onion, peeled and finely chopped
- 2 cloves garlic, peeled and minced
- 2 medium tomatoes, peeled and chopped
- 1 egg, beaten
- 1/2 teaspoon ground cinnamon
- 1/4 teaspoon ground nutmeg
- 1/4 teaspoon ground cumin, or to taste
- Salt and freshly ground black pepper, to taste
- 1/2 pound mozzarella cheese, shredded, divided

Trim ends of eggplants; slice eggplants in half lengthwise. Cook in lightly salted boiling water 8 minutes, or until just fork tender. Drain well and set aside to cool.

Brown lamb in a medium skillet. Drain off all fat; return lamb to skillet. Add onion, garlic and tomatoes; mix well. Cook over medium heat 4 minutes, stirring occasionally. Spoon meat mixture into a medium bowl.

Hollow out cooled eggplant halves, leaving 1/2-inch thick shells and saving pulp. Remove and discard seeds, then chop pulp and add it to lamb mixture. Stir in egg, cinnamon, nutmeg, cumin, salt, pepper and half of the mozzarella cheese. Spoon mixture into eggplant shells.

Place shells, filled-side up, in a medium baking dish. Sprinkle with remaining cheese. Bake, uncovered, in a preheated 350-degree oven 30 to 35 minutes, or until cheese is lightly browned.

East Indian Lamb Curry

Lori Longbotham
Food Editor, *New York Post*, New York City, New York

Here's an exotic meal with no exotic ingredients; you can purchase everything at the supermarket. Make this with either lamb or beef; the lamb cooks a little faster. Serve either with rice. It's a complete meal that's low in fat and calories — so you can really enjoy it.

Makes 4 servings

- 6 tablespoons vegetable oil, divided
- 2 medium onions, peeled and coarsely chopped
- 1/3 cup sliced almonds
- 1 tablespoon minced fresh ginger
- 5 small cloves garlic, peeled and chopped
- 1 teaspoon ground cumin seeds
- 1/2 teaspoon ground coriander
- 1/2 teaspoon ground cardamom
- 1-1/2 cups beef broth
- 3/4 cup plain non-fat or low-fat yogurt
- 2 pounds lean boneless lamb from the leg or rib (or 2 pounds boneless beef round), cut into 1x1/2-inch pieces
- 4 small red potatoes, pared and diced
- 8 ounces fresh green beans, trimmed and cut into 1-inch lengths
- 3 tablespoons minced fresh cilantro or parsley
- Hot cooked rice

Heat 3 tablespoons oil in a large, heavy-bottomed skillet with a lid over medium-high heat. Add onions; cook, stirring constantly, about 8 minutes, or until browned. Add almonds, ginger and garlic; cook, stirring constantly, over medium heat for 5 minutes. Add cumin, ground coriander and cardamom; cook, stirring, for 1 minute.

Transfer onion mixture to a food processor or blender; puree. Add beef broth and yogurt; process until smooth.

Heat remaining 3 tablespoons oil over medium heat in the same skillet. Brown meat in batches, about 3 minutes for each batch. After cooking all the meat, return it all to the skillet. Add pureed onion mixture, potatoes and green beans; stir to combine. Bring to a boil. Reduce heat and simmer, covered, for 20 to 25 minutes, stirring occasionally. Garnish with minced cilantro. Serve hot over rice.

Alligator Sauce Piquante

Betty W. Bernard
Food Editor, *Lake Charles American Press*, Lake Charles, Louisiana

It's been said that a real Cajun will eat anything that grows in the ground, runs or crawls over the land, flies in the air or swims in the sea. Many Cajuns schedule their vacations to coincide with the opening of shrimp and oyster season, or hunting seasons.

In southwestern Louisiana, there also is a season for hunting alligators. Once hunted only for their hides, alligators have a mild, white meat that is now considered a delicacy. Frozen alligator meat is shipped to food specialty stores across the country. It can be fried, barbecued, ground for meat balls or patties, or cut into pieces for soups, stews and gumbos. I'm particularly fond of this recipe, which is a thick stew flavored with tomatoes and usually served over rice.

Makes 6 servings

3 pounds alligator meat (see note)
Dollop of bottled steak sauce
1/2 cup solid vegetable shortening, divided
1-1/4 cups all-purpose flour
3 large onions, peeled and chopped
1 large green bell pepper, seeded and chopped
1/2 cup chopped green onions
8 ribs celery, chopped
1 can (8 ounces) tomato sauce
1 can (6 ounces) tomato paste
1 tablespoon cayenne pepper, or to taste
1 cup water
Salt (optional)
Hot cooked rice

Chop alligator meat into small strips; add a dollop of steak sauce, to coat. Heat some of the shortening in a large saucepot or Dutch oven; add alligator and brown. Remove meat; set aside.

Add remaining shortening and flour; mix well. Add onion, green pepper, green onion and celery; saute slowly until vegetables are tender. Add tomato sauce and tomato paste; mix well. Add cayenne pepper and water. Cover and cook over medium heat for 30 minutes. Stir in reserved alligator meat. Cook 1 hour, or until meat is tender. Add salt to taste. Serve over cooked rice.

Note: Any fowl or seafood can be used in place of the alligator meat.

Tarragon Veal Stew

Lori Longbotham
Food Editor, *New York Post*, New York City, New York

This stew has a fancy French flavor, but no fancy ingredients — they all come from the supermarket. The tarragon and mustard really make the stew sparkle and give it a clean, fresh taste. Serve this stew anytime of the year — it's always appropriate. I like to serve it with noodles, but you might prefer it with rice — try it both ways.

Makes 4 servings

- 4 tablespoons unsalted butter, divided
- 2 medium onions, peeled and diced
- 2 shallots, peeled and minced
- 2 pounds veal leg or shoulder, cut into 1-inch cubes
- 1/2 cup all-purpose flour
- 1/2 cup apple juice
- 1 can (14-1/2 ounces) chicken broth
- 4 small carrots, peeled and thinly sliced
- 2 teaspoons minced fresh tarragon or 1 teaspoon dried tarragon
- 2 teaspoons Dijon-style mustard
- Salt and freshly ground black pepper, to taste

Melt 2 tablespoons butter in a large Dutch oven over medium heat. Add onions and shallots; cook, stirring occasionally, about 5 minutes, or until softened. Remove to a plate.

Coat veal cubes with flour. Melt remaining 2 tablespoons butter in pan; add veal in batches and saute each batch about 5 minutes, or until lightly browned on all sides. Add veal to plate.

Pour apple juice into pan; cook 1 to 2 minutes, scraping up any browned bits on bottom. Return veal and onions to pan; stir in chicken broth and carrots. Cook, uncovered, stirring frequently, over medium-low heat about 45 minutes, or until veal is tender.

Stir in tarragon and mustard. Season with salt and pepper. Serve hot with noodles or rice.

Microwave method: Melt butter in a 3-quart microwave-safe baking dish on High (100 percent) power about 1 minute. Add onions and shallots; stir to coat. Microwave on High, covered, 4 minutes, stirring once.

Coat veal cubes with flour; add to onions. Microwave on High, covered, 9 minutes, stirring twice. Pour in apple juice and chicken broth. Microwave on Medium (50 percent) power, covered, 30 minutes. Stir in carrots. Microwave, covered, on Medium power for 10 minutes. Stir in tarragon and mustard. Season with salt and pepper. Serve hot with noodles and rice.

Liver Fricassee

Florence D. Roggenbach
Food Editor, *Norfolk Daily News*, Norfolk, Nebraska

My mother's family came to this country from Germany. That background influenced many of the recipes she prepared. Before you turn up your nose at this recipe, try it. It's one of our family's favorites.

Makes 6 to 8 servings

2 cups boiling water
1 pound beef liver
1/4 cup all-purpose flour
1/2 teaspoon salt, or to taste
1/8 teaspoon ground black pepper
2 to 3 slices bacon
1 can (14-1/2 ounces) whole tomatoes, drained and cut into bite-size pieces
3 medium green bell peppers, seeded and chopped
6 small white onions, peeled and chopped
1/2 teaspoon celery salt
1/2 teaspoon poultry seasoning
3 cups cooked egg noodles

Pour boiling water over liver in a dish; let stand 5 minutes. Drain liver, reserving water. Pat liver dry with paper towels. Cut liver into 12 to 16 pieces. Combine flour, salt and pepper; dredge liver in flour mixture.

Fry bacon in a large skillet. Remove cooked bacon from skillet, leaving fat in skillet. Drain bacon on paper towels. When bacon is cool, crumble and set aside. Quickly brown dredged liver in hot bacon fat in skillet. Add tomatoes, green peppers, onions, reserved crumbled bacon and reserved water from liver. Add celery salt and poultry seasoning. Cover and simmer 45 minutes.

Serve liver and vegetables over cooked noodles.

Green Chili Pork

Lori Longbotham
Food Editor, *New York Post,* New York City, New York

This one-dish meal has terrific Southwestern flavors. It's simple and quick to prepare, but it's not too spicy, which means both adults and kids will enjoy it. My favorite way to serve it is with flour tortillas, lime wedges and sour cream. If you're concerned about the fat in your diet, try light sour cream or low-fat yogurt.

Makes 6 servings

- 3 tablespoons vegetable oil
- 3 pounds pork loin, cut into 1-inch cubes
- 1 large onion, peeled and coarsely chopped
- 1 red bell pepper, seeded and diced
- 1 green bell pepper, seeded and diced
- 2 cloves garlic, peeled and minced
- 1 fresh jalapeño pepper, seeded and minced
- 1/2 teaspoon dried oregano
- 1/2 teaspoon ground cumin
- 1/4 cup water
- 1 tablespoon vinegar
- 1-1/2 teaspoons salt, or to taste
- 1/2 cup minced fresh cilantro, divided
- 2 cans (4 ounces each) chopped mild green chilies, drained
- Flour tortillas
- Lime wedges
- Dairy sour cream (or light sour cream or plain yogurt)

Heat oil in a large Dutch oven over medium heat. Add pork in batches and cook each batch about 4 minutes, or until browned on all sides. Using a slotted spoon, remove pork to a plate.

Add onion, red and green bell peppers, garlic, jalapeño pepper, oregano and cumin to pan; mix well. Cook, stirring occasionally, about 5 minutes, or until vegetables are softened. Return pork to pan; add water, vinegar, salt and half the cilantro. Simmer, uncovered, over very low heat for 1 to 1-1/2 hours, or until pork is tender. Stir in remaining cilantro and green chilies.

Serve hot with warm flour tortillas, lime wedges and sour cream.

Microwave method: Drizzle oil over pork in a 3-quart microwave-safe baking dish; stir to coat. Microwave, covered, on High (100 percent) power 8 minutes, stirring once. Stir in onion, red and green bell peppers, garlic, jalapeño pepper, oregano and cumin. Microwave on High, covered, 4 minutes.

Stir in water, vinegar and salt. Microwave, covered, on Medium (50 percent) power 40 minutes. Add cilantro and green chilies; stir to combine. Taste and adjust seasonings.

Serve hot with warm flour tortillas, lime wedges and sour cream.

Sausage Dip

Teri Grimes

Food Editor, *The Bradenton Herald*, Bradenton, Florida

This is one of the recipes I like to feature as a dip at any festive, informal gathering in our family. It's almost like a one-pot beef Stroganoff, using sausage instead of beef. However, it could be served in baked patty shells, as an interesting appetizer at a sit-down dinner.

Makes 3-1/2 to 4 cups

1 pound bulk pork sausage (spicy is best)
1 medium onion, peeled and finely chopped (about 1/2 cup)
1/2 pound fresh mushrooms, thinly sliced
1-1/2 tablespoons all-purpose flour
1 cup dairy sour cream
1 cup milk
1 tablespoon Worcestershire sauce
1 teaspoon soy sauce
1 teaspoon paprika
Corn chips, for dipping

In a 12-inch skillet, cook sausage until well browned, crumbling it with a fork. Remove sausage with a slotted spoon to paper towels to drain.

Add onions and mushrooms to the fat in the skillet; cook rapidly (so mushrooms will not give off their liquid), stirring often, until onion is golden brown. Drain off fat. Return sausage to skillet.

In a small bowl, gradually whisk flour into sour cream to make a smooth mixture. Whisk in milk, Worcestershire sauce, soy sauce and paprika; add to sausage mixture and mix well. Cook over moderate heat, stirring constantly, until thickened. Do not boil.

Serve hot in a chafing dish, with corn chips as dippers.

Chinese-Style Pork Chops with Three Mushrooms

Jane Witty Gould
Food Editor, *The Daily Journal*, Elizabeth, New Jersey

One of the greatest boons to home cooks has been the virtual explosion of specialty produce. Neighborhood supermarkets are now the source of exotic vegetables that were found only in gourmet groceries.

Mushroom lovers in particular have drawn an embarrassment of riches. While shoppers formerly had to content themselves with the cultivated variety, they now can have their favorite fungi in wild profusion: meaty black shiitakes, slender white enoki or funnel-shaped golden chanterelles. If your supermarket allows customers the option of weighing out their own mushrooms from bulk baskets, it is a good idea to mix a few ounces of several varieties. The many varieties of mushrooms have helped me create inspired spur-of-the-moment dishes, such as this one.

Makes 4 to 6 servings

- 5 tablespoons peanut oil, divided
- 1 clove garlic, peeled
- 3 slices fresh ginger
- 6 rib pork chops, 1/2-inch thick
- 1 tablespoon Chinese rice vinegar
- 1/2 cup strong, flavorful chicken broth
- 1/4 pound mixed chanterelle and shiitake mushrooms, stemmed and sliced
- 3 large cultivated (button) mushrooms, sliced
- 1 tablespoon oyster sauce
- 1 tablespoon hoisin sauce

In a 12-inch skillet, heat 4 tablespoons peanut oil until medium hot. Add garlic clove and ginger slices. Saute 30 seconds, or until they release their flavor, but do not brown. Discard garlic and ginger, reserving flavored oil.

Saute pork chops, three at a time, in the flavored oil until nicely browned on both sides; remove chops to a plate.

Add rice vinegar to skillet. Stir to scrape up brown bits. Add chicken broth; simmer until reduced slightly.

Meanwhile, heat the remaining 1 tablespoon oil in a medium skillet. Saute the three kinds of mushrooms over high heat until they color slightly and begin to release their juices. Add oyster sauce and hoisin sauce to mushrooms; stir well.

Return chops to broth mixture in large skillet. Scatter mushroom mixture over all. Cover and simmer on low heat for 12 minutes, or just until tender.

Harvest Sweet Potato Meat Pie

Judy Johnson
Food Editor, *Mississippi Press*, Pascagoula, Mississippi

Mississippi farmers grow some of the sweetest yams (sweet potatoes) in the South and market them throughout the country. Their golden delicious goodness is made to order for casseroles, such as this one that originally was developed by the Mississippi Sweet Potato Council. As we say down home: It's yam good, y'all!

Makes 6 servings

- 2 pounds sweet potatoes, cooked and cut into thick slices
- 3 tablespoons margarine or butter
- 1/2 teaspoon orange extract
- 1/4 cup evaporated milk
- 1/2 pound bulk pork sausage
- 12 ounces cooked ham
- 1 can (10-count) refrigerated butter-tasting biscuits (such as Hungry Jack)

In a large bowl, combine sweet potatoes, margarine, orange extract and evaporated milk; mix.

Cook sausage in a skillet, breaking it into small pieces as it cooks; pour off fat.

Cut ham into thin slices.

Separate biscuits; arrange close together on work surface. Roll out biscuits, pressing edges together to make one solid piece; roll out to pie crust thickness. Use a little more than half the dough to line a 12x7x2-inch casserole dish. Make a layer of ham slices, then a layer of half the potato mixture, then the sausage and then the remaining potato mixture. Top with remaining dough to make a top crust; seal edges. Cut vents in top crust. Bake in a preheated 350-degree oven for 30 minutes.

Austrian-Style Ragout Soup with Bread Dumplings

Adelaide A. Patten
Food Writer, *The Press of Atlantic City*, Pleasantville, New Jersey

During a trip to Austria several years ago, I visited a small village restaurant where my palate renewed its acquaintance with Ragout Soup served with feather-light bread dumplings. The meal evoked fond memories of a family staple on my grandmother's and mother's tables. On my return to the United States, I tried to recreate the dish. This resulting recipe rolled back the years for me. The secret of the soup's wonderful taste is using broth made from veal bones.

Makes 4 to 6 servings

1 pound veal bones
2 quarts cold water
5 tablespoons unsalted butter, divided
1/2 pound boneless veal, cut into small pieces
1 tablespoon chopped fresh parsley
1/4 cup all-purpose flour
1 cup green peas (fresh or frozen)
1/2 cup cut asparagus (1/2-inch pieces)
4 to 6 asparagus tips
1 egg
2 tablespoons heavy cream
Salt and black pepper, to taste
1/2 teaspoon imported sweet paprika
Bread dumplings (recipe follows)

Place veal bones in a soup kettle. Add water; bring to a boil. Reduce heat and simmer for 1-1/2 hours, skimming scum from surface as it forms.

Remove kettle from heat; remove bones. If bones are meaty, remove all meat and add meat to broth in kettle. Discard bones.

Melt 1 tablespoon butter in a skillet over medium heat. Add veal and saute 15 minutes, stirring frequently. Add chopped parsley; cook 5 minutes, stirring occasionally.

Return kettle of veal broth to medium heat. Add sauteed veal mixture. Bring to a boil. Reduce heat; simmer 2 hours, or until veal is very tender.

In a small saucepan, melt the remaining 4 tablespoons butter over medium heat. Add flour and stir with a wooden spoon until all the flour is moistened. Cook, stirring constantly, until flour begins to turn pale tan in color. Immediately remove pan from heat. Using a whisk, briskly stir in 1 cup veal broth (from the soup kettle), a few tablespoons at a time. When the cup of broth has been added, continue cooking over medium heat for 2 minutes, stirring constantly. Gradually stir this mixture into the contents of the soup kettle and cook 5 minutes, stirring occasionally.

Cook peas and asparagus pieces and tips separately in a little water until barely tender. Add peas and asparagus pieces to soup kettle, reserving asparagus tips for garnish. Allow soup to heat 2 minutes. Remove from heat.

Beat egg in a small bowl until well mixed. Gradually beat in cream, then slowly add 1/2 cup hot soup. Add this mixture to soup kettle, stirring constantly.

Return kettle to low heat and cook 2 to 3 minutes, stirring constantly until soup thickens slightly. Add salt and pepper to taste; stir in paprika.

Put 3 to 4 bread dumplings in each heated soup bowl; ladle soup over dumplings. Garnish each serving with a reserved asparagus tip.

Bread Dumplings

Makes 12 to 24 Dumplings

- 2 tablespoons unsalted butter, melted and cooled
- 1 egg, well beaten
- Few grains freshly grated nutmeg
- 1 tablespoon finely chopped fresh parsley
- Salt and black pepper, to taste
- 1 cup dry bread crumbs (made from crustless dry white bread either grated or crushed by rolling pin)

With a fork, combine melted butter, beaten egg, nutmeg, parsley, salt and pepper. Work in enough bread crumbs to make a dough-like mass that can be shaped into balls the size of small walnuts by gently rolling bread mixture between your wet palms. Depending on the size of the egg, you might need less or more than the listed amount of bread crumbs.

Bring a deep skillet of salted water to simmering. Test one dumpling in the simmering water to see if it will stick together. If not, add a bit more bread crumbs and test again.

When dumpling mixture is adjusted, shape into balls as directed. Poach balls gently in simmering water. When dumplings float on the surface, they are cooked.

Remove dumplings carefully with a slotted spoon and drain on a plate covered with a white napkin. Handle carefully; the dumplings are light and fragile.

Hurry-Up Pork Chops

Beth Whitley Duke
Food Editor, *Amarillo Globe-News*, Amarillo, Texas

Pork chops layered over potatoes in a rich, sour cream sauce won't help your diet, but the dish will warm up chilly autumn night suppers. I call it Hurry-Up Pork Chops because I like to pre-cook the potatoes in the microwave oven until they begin to soften before I add a layer of thinly sliced pork chops. For best results, add the sour cream mixture during the last 15 minutes of baking so it will retain its rich consistency.

Makes 4 servings

4 medium baking potatoes
1 pound thinly sliced pork chops
1 medium onion, peeled and sliced
1 carton (8 ounces) dairy sour cream (or plain yogurt)
1 envelope (about 1 ounce) dry onion soup mix

Spray a 13x9x2-inch glass baking dish with non-stick vegetable spray. Peel potatoes; slice into the bottom of prepared dish, making a thick layer. If desired, partly cook potatoes in a microwave oven at 80 percent power for about 8 minutes. If you prefer conventional cooking, add 1/2 cup water to potatoes and bake in a preheated 350-degree oven for about 10 minutes.

After partly cooking potatoes, top them with pork chops and cover chops with onion slices. Bake in a preheated 350-degree oven for 30 minutes.

In a small bowl, combine sour cream and dry soup mix. Spread evenly over pork chop mixture. Return to oven and bake 15 minutes. Serve hot.

Seafood

66 He Stew

67 Tuna Casserole

68 Jiffy Scallop Casserole

69 Dilled Seafood Medley

70 Creole Seafood Supreme

71 Barbecued Shrimp

72 Riviera Sole

73 Baked Halibut with Orange and Sun-Dried Tomatoes

74 Florida Paella

75 Back Burner Artichoke-Oyster Soup

76 Louisiana Crawfish Casserole

77 Mullet Stew

78 Buttermilk Bay Clam Chowder

79 Thick and Hearty Fish Soup

80 Creole Shrimp with Fettuccine Meunière

81 Frogmore Stew

82 Crab Royale

83 Catfish Caribbean

84 Mexican-Style Snapper with Lime

85 Tin Can Casserole

86 Portuguese-Style Boatman's Stew

He Stew

Sara Anne Corrigan
Food Editor, *The Evansville Press*, Evansville, Indiana

The following recipe was developed by my brother from the text of James Michener's 1978 novel, Chesapeake. *I refined it a bit further, because my brother wasn't much better at calculating exact measurements than Michener.*

The original version of the recipe can be found on pages 847 and 848 of the Fawcett Crest paperback edition of the book. It is written in the dialect of an uneducated black man, a cook aboard an oyster boat, who explains that the difference between "he" stew and "she" stew has nothing to do with the gender of oysters, rather it refers to the gender of the eaters.

The story makes great table conversation prior to serving up this incredibly rich and delicious dish. "He Stew" might be what the Chesapeake watermen prefer, but at our house, it's referred to as "we stew."

The only significant differences between this recipe and the one in Michener's text (other than volume—we have no need to feed an entire crew) are using cornstarch as a thickening agent rather than the "powdered tapioca" called for in the original, and reducing the amount of butter — the text calls for half a pound. We halved that amount, but it could be eliminated completely.

Makes 8 to 10 servings

1 pound bacon
2 cups chopped onion
2 cups chopped celery
2 pints raw oysters, drained, liquor reserved
4 cups milk, half-and-half or heavy cream, as desired
2 tablespoons cornstarch
Salt and black pepper (optional)
Healthy pinch of saffron
1/2 cup butter
Oyster crackers

Fry bacon until crisp; drain on paper towels. Reserve drippings. Crumble bacon; set aside. In a large skillet or Dutch oven, use some of the reserved bacon drippings to saute onion and celery until soft. Remove vegetables from pan.

Drain liquor from oysters and reserve. Saute oysters in pan drippings just until they start to curl.

Heat milk; whisk in cornstarch that has been dissolved in a small amount of reserved oyster liquor. Simmer, stirring, until mixture becomes very thick and gelatinous, adding more cornstarch, if needed. Add oysters and vegetables. Add remaining oyster liquor as needed to maintain a smooth, creamy consistency as the stew cooks, uncovered, over low heat for 15 minutes. Taste; add salt and pepper, if desired.

At serving time, transfer stew to serving bowl. Grind saffron to a powder and sprinkle evenly over top of stew. Cut butter in half; nestle pieces into top of stew. Sprinkle reserved crumbled bacon over all. Serve with oyster crackers.

Tuna Casserole

Ann C. Wells

Food Editor, *The Grand Rapids Press*, Grand Rapids, Michigan

Most tuna casseroles are boring fare, but not this version. It was created years ago by my close friend, Susan Doyle Lipner, to show her home economics class that tuna casserole is not just a mixture of tuna, mushroom soup and macaroni, and that casserole recipes can be easily adapted to use other ingredients. This is wonderful for dinner, but it also makes a different and tasty brunch dish. Best of all, it's made in one dish.

Makes 4 to 6 servings

- 1 cup dairy sour cream
- 1/4 teaspoon dried oregano
- 2 cans (6-1/2 ounces each) water-packed tuna, drained
- 1/2 cup sliced ripe olives
- 3/4 cup canned sliced mushrooms, drained (or 3/4 cup sliced fresh mushrooms, lightly sauteed)
- 1/4 to 1/2 cup cashews
- Grated Cheddar cheese

In a 1-1/2 quart casserole dish, combine sour cream, oregano, tuna, olives, mushrooms and cashews. Sprinkle with grated cheese. Bake in a preheated 350-degree oven for 25 to 30 minutes, or until hot and bubbly.

Jiffy Scallop Casserole

Judy Johnson
Food Editor, *Mississippi Press*, Pascagoula, Mississippi

Scallops are a sweet treat, and here on the Gulf Coast we like to cook them in a casserole that keeps well and shows off nicely for company. This recipe was developed by Joyce Clanton with Florida's Department of Natural Resources. It has become one of my personal favorites. It can be used with either bay scallops or calico scallops found in Florida waters or with scallops harvested from other American waters.

Makes 6 serving

- 2 pounds bay scallops, fresh or frozen
- 1 quart water
- 2 tablespoons salt, or less if desired
- 1 can (16 ounces) cut green beans, drained
- 1/4 cup chopped onion
- 3 tablespoons vegetable oil, divided
- 1 can (10-3/4 ounces) condensed cream of mushroom soup, undiluted
- 1/2 cup milk
- 1 teaspoon curry powder
- 1/8 teaspoon black pepper
- 1/2 cup crushed cracker crumbs
- 1/4 cup grated Cheddar cheese

Thaw scallops, if frozen. Rinse with cold water to remove any shel particles. Combine 1 quart water and salt in a 2-quart saucepan an bring to a boil. Add scallops; reduce heat and cover. Simmer for 2 t 3 minutes, depending on the size of the scallops. Drain.

In a well-greased 8x8x2-inch baking dish, combine cooked scal lops and green beans; set aside.

In a medium saucepan, saute onion in 2 tablespoons oil until tender Add soup, milk, curry powder and pepper. Heat, stirring, until wel blended. Pour soup mixture over scallop mixture.

Combine crumbs, cheese and remaining 1 tablespoon oil. Sprinkl over top of casserole. Bake in a preheated 425-degree oven for 10 t 15 minutes.

Dilled Seafood Medley

Barbara Bloch
President, *International Cookbook Services*, White Plains, New York

You can prepare this casserole in the morning and set it aside in the refrigerator until you are ready to bake it. If the casserole is cold, rather than at room temperature, you might have to increase the baking time by 5 to 10 minutes. If desired, serve Seafood Medley over rice, with a crisp green vegetable and warm garlic bread.

Makes 4 to 6 servings

- 4 tablespoons butter or margarine
- 1 pound medium shrimp, shelled and deveined
- 1/2 pound flounder fillets, cubed
- 1/4 pound bay scallops
- 1/2 pound fresh mushrooms, sliced
- 1 medium onion, peeled and chopped
- 2 tablespoons all-purpose flour
- 1 cup light cream or milk
- 1/4 cup grated Parmesan cheese
- 2 tablespoons Dijon-style mustard
- 1 teaspoon freshly snipped dill or 1/4 teaspoon dried dill weed
- Salt and freshly ground black pepper, to taste
- Seasoned dry bread crumbs
- Paprika
- Fresh dill sprigs, for garnish

Melt butter in a large skillet. Add shrimp, flounder, scallops, mushrooms and onion. Saute 5 minutes, or until shrimp are pink and onion is transparent. Remove with slotted spoon and place in a 2-quart casserole dish; set side.

Add flour to liquid in skillet, stir into liquid and cook 2 minutes. Add cream slowly, stirring constantly; cook until sauce begins to thicken. Stir in cheese, mustard, snipped dill, salt and pepper. Cook until cheese is melted.

Spoon sauce over seafood in casserole. Sprinkle with bread crumbs and paprika. Bake, uncovered, in a preheated 350-degree oven 30 minutes, or until top is golden brown. Garnish with dill sprigs.

Creole Seafood Supreme

Carolyn Flournoy
Food Columnist, *The Times,* Shreveport, Louisiana

This is an old south Louisiana recipe that I have adapted for my own use. It is expensive, but well worth the investment. I believe it is the best seafood casserole I have ever tasted. Paired with a marinated vegetable salad and garlic bread, it makes an impressive meal for a dinner party. Guests always ask for the recipe—and if you're smart you won't give it out because they're apt to serve it at their next dinner party.

Makes 10 to 12 servings

1 package (8 ounces) cream cheese
1/2 cup butter, divided
1-1/2 pounds raw shrimp, peeled
6 to 7 green onions, sliced
1 small red bell pepper, seeded and chopped
3 ribs celery, thinly sliced
1 can (10-3/4 ounces) condensed cream of mushroom soup, undiluted
1 jar (6 ounces) sliced mushrooms, drained
1 teaspoon hot pepper sauce
1 teaspoon garlic salt, or to taste
1 teaspoon Worcestershire sauce
1/2 teaspoon cayenne pepper
1 pound crab meat
1 tablespoon lemon juice
3 cups cooked rice
2-1/2 cups grated Cheddar cheese
Cracker crumbs
Paprika

Melt cream cheese and 6 tablespoons butter in the top of a double boiler or microwave oven; set aside.

Saute shrimp, green onions, bell pepper and celery in remaining 2 tablespoons butter.

In a large bowl, combine mushroom soup, mushrooms, hot pepper sauce, garlic salt, Worcestershire sauce and cayenne pepper. Add cream cheese mixture and sauteed shrimp mixture; stir to combine. Sprinkle crab meat with lemon juice; carefully stir into shrimp mixture. Stir in cooked rice.

Spoon into a greased 3-quart rectangular casserole dish. Top with cheese, then sprinkle with cracker crumbs and paprika. Bake in a preheated 350-degree oven for 30 minutes, or until heated through and bubbly.

Barbecued Shrimp

Carolyn Flournoy
Food Columnist, *The Times,* Shreveport, Louisiana

This recipe is thought to have originated at Manale's Restaurant in New Orleans. Why they call it Barbecued Shrimp, only one long-gone chef would know. Every good Louisiana cook has a version of it in their repertoire. This is mine. Serve the shrimp and sauce in large soup or gumbo bowls with plenty of crusty French bread for dunking. Add a tossed salad and you have a memorable meal.

Because your guests have to peel the shrimp at the table, this recipe is best served with lots of napkins. I sometimes cover the table with newspaper. If you don't want to do that, use a paper tablecloth. Be sure to place extra bowls on the table for the shells.

Makes 8 to 10 servings

5 pounds unpeeled shrimp
1-1/2 cups butter
1 bottle (8 ounces) Italian salad dressing
1/3 cup lemon juice
1/4 cup olive oil
2 to 3 cloves garlic, peeled and minced
1/2 teaspoon hot pepper sauce
2 to 3 tablespoons ground black pepper, or more to taste
1 tablespoon Worcestershire sauce

Wash shrimp and drain well.

Melt butter in a 3-quart casserole dish while you are preheating oven to 350 degrees. Add salad dressing, lemon juice, olive oil, garlic, hot pepper sauce, black pepper and Worcestershire sauce to butter; stir to combine. Add shrimp.

Bake, covered, in preheated 350-degree oven for 35 to 45 minutes, stirring occasionally so all shrimp cook evenly. Shrimp turn bright pink when done; be sure all are completely cooked.

Note: This dish is equally good reheated, but it should not be frozen. Recipe can be halved, using 2-1/2 pounds unpeeled shrimp and adjusting other ingredients.

Riviera Sole

Ann C. Wells
Food Editor, *The Grand Rapids Press,* Grand Rapids, Michigan

While trying to work more fish into my family's meals, I dug back into my files and found this recipe that I had only tried once. I remembered it was delicious, but because I don't really like fish, I never made it again. This past year it has become a favorite way to prepare fish. It makes an easy, but elegant, company entree. I changed the original recipe to use fresh and more healthful ingredients.

Makes 6 servings

1 cup plain yogurt
1/2 cup low-calorie, cholesterol-free mayonnaise
1 tablespoon lemon juice
1/2 teaspoon curry powder
2 pounds sole fillets
Salt and black pepper, to taste
4 ounces fresh mushroom caps, lightly sauteed
1 can (16 or 17 ounces) green grapes, drained, or about 2 cups fresh seedless green grapes

In a small bowl, combine yogurt, mayonnaise, lemon juice and curry powder. Spread half of the yogurt mixture on the fish fillets; season with salt and pepper to taste. Roll up fillets and secure with toothpicks.

Spray a 13x9x2-inch baking dish with non-stick cooking spray. Place fish rolls in baking dish. Pour remaining yogurt mixture over them. Top with sauteed mushrooms and grapes. Bake in a preheated 350-degree oven for 30 minutes.

Note: This dish can be made in advance and refrigerated until baking time.

Baked Halibut with Orange and Sun-Dried Tomatoes

Jane Witty Gould
Food Editor, *The Daily Journal,* Elizabeth, New Jersey

Cafe Luxembourg, on Manhattan's Upper West Side, was one of the earliest proponents of consistently good new American cooking. Although trendy, the combinations were never bizarre.

Several years ago at the cafe, I had a dish of poached halibut with tomato coulis that was subtly flavored with oranges. The sweet citrus and the acid tomatoes brought out the delicacy of the halibut without overpowering it. At home I worked with this trio of flavors until I arrived at this simple baked version.

Makes 2 servings

2 halibut steaks, 1-inch thick (8 to 9 ounces each)
2 tablespoons olive oil, divided
Salt and freshly ground black pepper, to taste
1/2 teaspoon dried rosemary
Rind and juice of 1 orange (Valencia, if available)
12 sun-dried tomatoes, rinsed and patted dry
1 shallot, peeled and chopped
2 tablespoons chopped fresh parsley, for garnish

Rinse halibut in cold water; pat dry. Drizzle 1 tablespoon olive oil in the bottom of an 11x9x2-inch oval gratin dish or similar baking dish. Season both sides of the fish with salt and pepper; sprinkle evenly with rosemary. Place fish in one layer in dish.

Sprinkle orange rind on top of fish. Pour orange juice around the fish. Scatter tomatoes and chopped shallot around fish. Drizzle with remaining 1 tablespoon olive oil.

Place dish on bottom rack of a preheated 450-degree oven. Bake exactly 15 minutes for moist fish. Remove and garnish with parsley.

Florida Paella

Mary Denise Scourtes
Food Writer, *The Tampa Tribune*, Tampa, Florida

One of the most famous dishes in Spain and in Florida's Spanish restaurants is paella. The rice-based stew of saffron, chicken, seafood and sausage is named for the two-handled, rather shallow cooking vessel named paellaera, from which it is served.

The method you use to make paella depends upon your teacher, because there are as many recipes for it as there are castanets in Spain. All agree, however, that real paella has to be made with saffron, the world's most expensive spice. Using saffron threads, rather than powder, is advisable, because the threads give the dish its distinctive punch.

Makes 8 servings

2 tablespoons olive oil
1 clove garlic
1 frying chicken, cut into serving pieces
1 chorizo (spicy, Spanish-style sausage), 6 to 8 ounces
3 tomatoes, chopped
1 onion, peeled and chopped
1 red bell pepper, seeded and chopped
1 teaspoon paprika
Salt and black pepper, to taste
1 fresh artichoke, cut into eighths, with tough outer edges removed
3 cups chicken broth
1 cup tomato sauce
2 cups rice, uncooked
1-1/2 teaspoons saffron threads, soaked in warm water
1 pound raw shrimp, peeled
1 cup green peas (fresh or frozen)
12 large Spanish olives
12 scallops
2 tablespoons chopped pimento
Fresh parsley
Fresh lemon wedges

Heat oil in a large, heavy iron skillet or paella pan. Add garlic and cook a few minutes; remove and reserve garlic.

In the same skillet, brown chicken and chorizo; drain fat. Add tomatoes, onion, bell pepper, paprika, salt, pepper and artichoke pieces to chicken and chorizo. Cook 10 minutes. Add chicken broth and tomato sauce. Bring to a boil. Add rice and saffron. Reduce heat and simmer, uncovered, 15 to 20 minutes.

Add shrimp, peas, olives, scallops, pimentos and reserved garlic. Cook 2 to 3 minutes, or until shrimp is cooked.

Garnish with parsley and lemon wedges.

Back Burner Artichoke-Oyster Soup

Betty W. Bernard

Food Editor, *Lake Charles American Press*, Lake Charles, Louisiana

The popularity of Cajun foods that has spread across the country recently attests to the cooking ability of the people in south Louisiana. But some restaurants in other states take advantage of the Cajun name. They simply add a lot of cayenne pepper or Louisiana hot sauce to regular dishes and call them Cajun.

That's not Cajun. Real Cajun food is not hot enough to burn the tongue. The true taste of the Cajun flavor comes from a subtle blending of various seasonings and ingredients, such as in this recipe.

Makes 2 quarts; 8 generous servings

1/2 cup butter
3 large green onions with tops, chopped
3 ribs celery, finely chopped
3 large cloves garlic, peeled and finely chopped
3 tablespoons all-purpose flour
2 cans (14 ounces each) artichoke hearts, rinsed, drained and cut into quarters
1 quart chicken broth
1 tablespoon Worcestershire sauce
Cayenne pepper, to taste
Salt, to taste
1 quart shucked raw oysters, drained and chopped, liquor reserved
1 teaspoon granulated sugar
2 bay leaves
1 cup evaporated milk
1 cup whole milk

Melt butter in a large skillet; saute green onions, celery and garlic in butter. Sprinkle in flour; stir and mix well. Add artichokes, chicken broth, Worcestershire sauce, cayenne pepper and salt. Cook over low heat 1 hour. Add oysters and reserved oyster liquor, sugar and bay leaves. Simmer over low heat 10 minutes; do not boil. Stir in evaporated milk and whole milk. Remove from heat.

Refrigerate at least 8 hours. Reheat over low heat before serving.

Note: Soup can be made up to 3 days in advance of serving; keep refrigerated until ready to use.

Louisiana Crawfish Casserole

Betty W. Bernard
Food Editor, *Lake Charles American Press*, Lake Charles, Louisiana

This crawfish casserole is typical of those found in many Louisiana cookbooks. Crawfish is so popular in our area that students at Iowa High School in Iowa, Louisiana, studying Louisiana culture, came up with this prayer to be said before eating crawfish:

GRACE BEFORE A CRAWFISH MEAL

Bless us, O Lord, and these crawfish which we are about to enjoy.
Bless those who caught them, those who prepared them,
And give crawfish to those who have none.
We thank You, O God, for this wonderful world
And for all that You have put on it.
And we give You special thanks, O God,
For having put the Cajuns and the crawfish
Down in the same place. Amen.

Makes 6 servings

- 1 cup chopped onions
- 3/4 cup chopped green bell pepper
- 1 clove garlic, peeled and minced
- 2 tablespoons butter
- 1 pound peeled, deveined, raw crawfish tails
- 1 can (10-3/4 ounces) condensed cream of mushroom soup, undiluted
- 3 cups cooked rice
- 1 tablespoon chopped fresh parsley
- 1-1/2 tablespoons lemon juice
- 1-1/2 teaspoons salt, or to taste
- 1/4 teaspoon ground black pepper
- 1/4 teaspoon cayenne pepper
- 2 slices white bread
- 1/2 cup milk
- Paprika
- 1 cup grated Cheddar or Monterey Jack cheese

In a large skillet, saute onions, green pepper and garlic in butter until tender-crisp. Add crawfish tails; cook 3 minutes. Stir in soup, cooked rice, parsley, lemon juice, salt, black pepper and cayenne pepper; mix well. Soak bread in milk; add to crawfish mixture and mix well.

Spoon into a buttered, shallow 2-quart casserole dish. Sprinkle with paprika.

Bake in a preheated 350-degree oven for 30 minutes. Remove from oven, sprinkle cheese over top and return to oven to bake just until cheese melts.

Mullet Stew

Lorrie Guttman
Food Editor, *Tallahassee Democrat*, Tallahassee, Florida

Mullet is a fish commonly caught in the Gulf of Mexico, so it's plentiful and inexpensive in Tallahassee. It's usually fried, but smoked mullet is my favorite. I've also come to appreciate mullet prepared in other ways, such as in this stew that won a prize in a recipe contest my newspaper held. Other fish fillets can be substituted for the mullet.

Makes 6 to 8 servings

1 tablespoon olive oil
10 to 12 skinned and boned mullet fillets (2 to 3 pounds total)
Greek seasoning (such as Cavender's), to taste
1 large onion, peeled and chopped
2 green bell peppers, seeded and chopped
1 clove garlic, peeled and minced
1 can (28 ounces) whole tomatoes, drained
3 tablespoons vinegar
Hot cooked rice

Lightly grease a 12-inch skillet with olive oil. Cover the bottom with fish fillets. Add Greek seasoning, onion, bell peppers and garlic. Crush tomatoes; add to fish mixture. Add vinegar. Cover and simmer about 45 minutes.

Serve stew over hot cooked rice.

Buttermilk Bay Clam Chowder

Jane Witty Gould
Food Editor, *The Daily Journal*, Elizabeth, New Jersey

When my children were small, we used to spend lazy August weekends digging for quahogs (chowder clams) in the sand on the shores of Cape Cod's Buttermilk Bay.

Our rental house, like most, came equipped with a few mismatched dishes, some cracked cups and an old chipped enamel stew pot. Yet some of the best summer meals we have ever eaten emerged from that unpromising kitchen.

One labor of love, an impromptu clam chowder, has been in the family ever since. Although the original recipe comes from Bean Town, it is not a pure New Englander. As a Long Islander, my chowder fantasies always include tomatoes. But this chowder is a compromise: creamy like a true Bostonian chowder, but with flecks of fresh tomato.

Makes 4 to 6 servings

- 1 dozen medium-sized chowder clams in the shell, scrubbed and cleaned
- 1/2 cup butter
- 3 medium-large onions, peeled and chopped
- 2 boiling potatoes, peeled and diced
- 2 ripe medium tomatoes, peeled, seeded and chopped
- Salt and white pepper, to taste
- 1 bay leaf
- 1/2 teaspoon dried thyme
- 2 cups light cream or half-and-half

Steam clams in a large covered pot in a small amount of boiling water until they open. Take out the clams as they open and continue to steam the unopened ones a few minutes more. Discard any clams that do not open. Shuck clams, then chop and set aside. Reserve 2 cups clam broth from the top of the pan after any sand has settled on the bottom. (Add water, if necessary, to make 2 cups liquid.)

Wash and dry the pot. Melt butter in pot; saute onions gently until translucent, but not brown. Add potatoes. Toss to coat with butter; saute 1 to 2 minutes. Add tomatoes. Season with salt, pepper, bay leaf and thyme. Return chopped clams to pot along with reserved 2 cups clam broth. (Chowder can be made ahead to this point.)

Just before serving, heat to boiling, then reduce heat to simmer and stir in cream. Continue to cook over low heat until soup is hot. Do not boil.

Note: White, new potatoes hold their shape best in chowder.

Thick and Hearty Fish Soup

Barbara Bloch
President, *International Cookbook Services,* White Plains, New York

Sometimes it is difficult to tell the difference between a thick, hearty soup and a stew. One difference is that soup usually can be prepared more quickly than stew. But either can be served as a meal, accompanied by a tossed green salad and freshly baked biscuits or crisp French bread.

Makes 4 generous servings

- 3 tablespoons butter or margarine
- 2 ribs celery, diced
- 1 large onion, peeled and chopped
- 6 cups chicken broth
- 5 large potatoes, cubed
- Salt and freshly ground black pepper, to taste
- 1 package (10 ounces) frozen peas and carrots
- 1 package (10 ounces) frozen French-cut green beans
- 1 can (15 ounces) stewed tomatoes, broken up, undrained
- 1-1/4 pounds whitefish or cod fillets, cut into 1-inch cubes
- Dairy sour cream and dill sprigs, for garnish

Melt butter in a large, deep saucepot. Add celery and onion; cook until onion is transparent. Add chicken broth, potatoes, salt and pepper. Bring to a boil. Reduce heat, cover and cook over low heat 20 minutes. Add frozen vegetables, undrained tomatoes and fish. Cook, covered, about 8 minutes, or until vegetables are cooked and fish flakes easily.

Ladle into large soup bowls. Garnish with dollops of sour cream and dill sprigs.

Creole Shrimp with Fettuccine Meunière

Jane Witty Gould
Food Editor, *The Daily Journal*, Elizabeth, New Jersey

I swear my son chose Tulane University in New Orleans on purpose, to give his mother an excuse to check out the Cajun food scene at least twice a year.

The thought of his being down there with all those oysters and crawfish at his beck and call makes me positively green with envy (even though he assures me that frequent forays to the French Quarter are too expensive for a student's budget). Still, just being there holds the same fascination for a foodie that hanging out on Hollywood and Vine has for an aspiring actor.

When my son comes home on vacation we get another dividend—he always brings home a recipe or two. Because we cook together, it follows that many of these treasures end up in my recipe repertoire.

One Christmas we decided on shrimp with fettuccine for a main dish. He set about melting a block of butter and shaking in some Worcestershire sauce and hot sauce. I watched with amazement as he began creating a classic Creole meunière sauce, but he didn't realize it had a name. When I mentioned it, he shrugged and said, "It's just a little Southern sauce I saw my roommate do."

Makes 3 to 4 servings

- 7 tablespoons butter
- 1 tablespoon Worcestershire sauce
- Few drops hot pepper sauce (such as Tabasco)
- Few drops mild Louisiana hot sauce (such as Landry's)
- Few drops jalapeño sauce (such as Trappey's)
- Juice of 1/2 lemon
- 1/2 teaspoon fines herbes
- 1 bay leaf
- 1/2 teaspoon dried leaf thyme
- 2 to 3 tablespoons vegetable oil
- 1-1/4 pounds large shrimp, shelled and deveined
- 2 tablespoons chopped fresh parsley
- 1 pound spinach fettuccine, cooked

In a 1-quart saucepan, melt butter over very low heat. Add Worcestershire sauce, hot pepper sauce, mild hot sauce and jalapeño sauce to taste. Stir in lemon juice, fines herbes, bay leaf and thyme. Keep warm, but do not simmer.

Heat oil in a large 12-inch skillet. Saute shrimp in oil 3 to 4 minutes, or just until shrimp turn pink, stirring occasionally.

When shrimp are done, pour off all but 1 tablespoon liquid from skillet. Add warm butter sauce to skillet; remove and discard bay leaf. Blend butter sauce well with shrimp. Stir in parsley. Serve over cooked fettuccine.

Note: New Orleans has literally dozens of hot sauces from mild to incendiary. Because of the popularity of Cajun and Creole food, many of these sauces are now available in supermarkets or gourmet shops across the country.

Frogmore Stew

Anne Byrn

Food Editor, *Atlanta Journal-Constitution*, Atlanta, Georgia

Along the coast of South Carolina a seafood medley called Frogmore Stew is served. It doesn't contain frogs at all. This stew is made of fresh shrimp, corn and smoked sausage. It's sort of a southern version of the northern Atlantic coast crab and lobster boils. You can add fresh blue crab, red-skinned potatoes and even firm fillets of white fish, if desired. No matter what you add to the recipe, be sure to serve this stew with plenty of napkins.

Makes 8 servings

3 pounds Polish or other smoked sausage, cut in 1-1/2-inch pieces
2 large onions, peeled and chopped
2 lemons, sliced
Salt and black pepper, to taste
2 tablespoons seafood seasoning (or shellfish seasoning)
1/2 cup butter
16 ears of corn, shucked
3 pounds raw, unpeeled large shrimp

Put 2 gallons of water into a large stockpot; add sausage, onions, lemons, salt, pepper and seafood seasoning. Bring to a boil; simmer, uncovered, for 45 minutes. Add butter; let melt. Add corn to pot; cook about 10 minutes.

Add shrimp; cook 5 minutes, or until shrimp are pink. Drain; serve stew on a large platter.

Crab Royale

Betty W. Bernard
Food Editor, *Lake Charles American Press*, Lake Charles, Louisiana

There is an old saying that you only get to be a Cajun in one of three ways — "by birth, by the ring, or by the back door." In earlier times, the front door of a Cajun's home led into the parlor, which was used only on special occasions. The "back door" took you into the kitchen, the heart of the home, where the family cooked, ate and visited with friends.

I grew up in north Louisiana, a completely different world from the bayous and marshlands of south Louisiana. I first came to Cajun country some 40 years ago, when I graduated from college, to set up the parish (county) library in Ville Platte. I was doubtful about meeting the people because I didn't speak French (and at that time, many of the older Cajuns still didn't speak English), and I was a Baptist in Catholic country. However, the driver of our bookmobile told me not to worry. He said, if the Cajun people like you, you can tell because you'll be invited into the kitchen for coffee. And we were invited for coffee at every stop along all the back roads. The people in Evangeline Parish were the friendliest folks in all the world. So I suppose I became a Cajun by the "back door" first, then later by "the ring" when I married a Cajun from Opelousas.

This recipe from friends in Eunice, Louisiana, is classified as a main-dish stew.

Makes 6 servings

3 tablespoons butter
3 tablespoons all-purpose flour
2/3 cup heavy cream
2/3 cup chicken broth
2 cups cooked crab meat
1/2 cup sliced fresh mushrooms
1 egg, beaten
Salt and black pepper, to taste
Hot cooked rice

Melt butter in large saucepan; stir in flour. Slowly add cream and chicken broth, stirring constantly over low heat until mixture thickens. Add cooked crab meat and mushrooms. Slowly add beaten egg; stir until heated. Season with salt and pepper to taste.

Serve crab mixture over cooked rice.

Note: French bread is ideal with this dish.

Catfish Caribbean

Judy Johnson
Food Editor, *Mississippi Press*, Pascagoula, Mississippi

Mississippi farm-raised catfish is taking the nation by storm. Recipes such as this one, developed by The Catfish Institute and one of my personal favorites, are part of the reason.

Down South, many folks think it's against the law to serve catfish any way but straight-up: fried to a golden brown in deep fat and mounded on a platter surrounded by hush puppies. All that is changing as food experts, such as Craig Claiborne and Wolfgang Puck, discover the infinite variety of this delicate, firm-fleshed fish.

Makes 4 servings

- 2 tablespoons butter or margarine
- 1/4 cup chopped green bell pepper
- 4 tablespoons chopped onion, divided
- 1/4 cup chopped toasted almonds
- 1/2 cup fresh bread crumbs
- 1/4 teaspoon dried oregano
- 4 tablespoons fresh lime juice, divided
- 1 tablespoon chopped fresh cilantro (fresh coriander) or chopped parsley
- 1/2 teaspoon salt, or to taste
- 4 farm-raised catfish fillets
- 1/2 cup water
- 2 cloves garlic, peeled and crushed
- 1 bay leaf
- 1 teaspoon crushed red pepper flakes
- Lime peel

Melt butter in a large skillet. Add green pepper and 2 tablespoons onion. Saute until onion is transparent. Add almonds, bread crumbs, oregano, 1 tablespoon lime juice, cilantro and salt; mix well.

Spoon filling down center of each catfish fillet. Roll up and secure with a toothpick.

In a shallow baking dish, combine remaining 2 tablespoons onion, water, garlic, bay leaf, red pepper flakes and remaining 3 tablespoons lime juice. Place rolled-up catfish in mixture in dish.

Bake, uncovered, in a preheated 400-degree oven for 30 to 35 minutes, basting occasionally, until fish flakes easily. Remove catfish to serving platter. Garnish with strips of lime peel.

Mexican-Style Snapper with Lime

Teri Grimes
Food Editor, *The Bradenton Herald*, Bradenton, Florida

This dish combines two of the best aspects of Florida cooking: fresh fish and fresh citrus. Snapper is one of the most popular fish on local menus — and with good reason. This firm fish holds up well in this one-skillet treatment. The chopped tomatoes and lime wedges scattered across the white flesh of the snapper make a pretty dish.

Makes 6 servings

1/2 cup chopped green onions
1/4 cup butter or margarine
1/2 pound fresh tomatoes, diced
1/4 cup chopped green chilies
2 tablespoons chopped fresh parsley
1/8 teaspoon salt
1/8 teaspoon garlic salt (or 1 clove garlic, peeled and minced)
1/4 teaspoon grated lime peel
1/8 teaspoon ground black pepper
1-1/2 pounds fresh snapper fillets
12 lime wedges

In a large skillet, saute green onions in butter until tender. (Also saute minced garlic, if using fresh.)

Add tomatoes, chilies, parsley, salt, garlic salt, lime peel and black pepper; mix well. Bring mixture to a boil, reduce heat and simmer 5 minutes.

Add snapper to skillet; spoon sauce over fillets. Cover and simmer 10 minutes, or until fish flakes easily when tested with a fork.

Serve garnished with lime wedges.

Note: This recipe works just as well with any firm-fleshed fish.

Tin Can Casserole

Ann C. Wells
Food Editor, *The Grand Rapids Press,* Grand Rapids, Michigan

Vegetable-hating kids really go for this casserole. My now-grown nieces and nephews, who never saw a vegetable they liked, always requested this recipe when they came to our cottage on Lake Michigan in the summertime. They must not have known that there were vegetables hidden in the layers. It's easy to make ahead of time and have on hand ready to bake.

Makes 8 to 10 servings

- 4 cans (6-1/2 ounces each) water-packed tuna, drained and broken up, divided
- 1 cup chopped celery
- 1 medium onion, peeled and finely chopped
- 1 can (5 ounces) chow mein noodles
- 2 cans (10-3/4 ounces each) condensed cream of chicken soup, undiluted, divided
- 1 can (8 ounces) sliced water chestnuts, drained
- 1 can (4 ounces) sliced mushrooms, drained
- 1 can (14 ounces) chop suey vegetables with bamboo shoots or meatless chop suey, drained
- 1 cup sliced or slivered almonds or cashews

Place 2 cans of tuna in the bottom of a lightly greased 3-quart round casserole dish. Add, in layers, the celery, onion, noodles, 1 can of soup, remaining 2 cans of tuna, water chestnuts, mushrooms and chop suey vegetables. Spread remaining 1 can of soup over top. Sprinkle nuts over soup.

Bake, uncovered, in a preheated 350-degree oven for 1 hour, or until heated though and bubbly.

Portuguese-Style Boatman's Stew

Adelaide A. Patten
Food Writer, *The Press of Atlantic City,* Pleasantville, New Jersey

A rich-tasting fish stew always finds favor as either a main dinner dish or as a luncheon meal. Boatman's Stew is a classic Portuguese invention, but my version is quick and easy. It's good any time of year and is as tasty as it is colorful.

Makes 4 servings

2 pounds white-fleshed fish (cod, haddock, hake or scrod), skinned, boned and cut into steaks or fillets
1/4 teaspoon salt
1-1/2 cups chopped onion
1/3 cup olive oil
2-1/2 cups peeled, chopped tomatoes (or one 16-ounce can tomatoes, drained and crushed)
4 tablespoons tomato paste
Salt and black pepper, to taste
3/4 teaspoon crushed sweet red pepper (or 1 teaspoon imported sweet paprika)
2 tablespoons minced fresh parsley
3/4 cup white grape juice
1-1/2 cups fish broth or bottled clam broth
Granulated or brown sugar (optional)
French or Italian bread

Sprinkle fish with 1/4 teaspoon salt. Cover lightly and refrigerat at least 3 hours.

Saute onion in olive oil until browned, stirring constantly tc prevent scorching. Add tomatoes, tomato paste, salt, black pepper, rec pepper, parsley, white grape juice and fish broth. Stir to blend Simmer 30 minutes, stirring occasionally.

Drain fish. Add fish to stew; return to simmer and cook gently unti fish is opaque and flakes easily with a fork.

Taste; adjust seasonings. If mixture is too tart, stir in a bit of sugar

Cut 4 thick slices of bread; place one slice in each of 4 deep sou plates or bowls. Ladle hot stew over bread, dividing fish as equally a possible among bowls. Serve immediately. Pass extra bread so diner can blot up every last bit of the delicious sauce.

Cheese and Eggs

88 Hadassah Cheese Soufflé

89 Some Like It Hot Brunch Casserole

90 Egg Casserole

91 Crab Cheese Fondue

92 Christmas Brunch

93 Quiche Roquefort a la Canyon

94 California Frittata

95 Cheese-Rice Casserole

96 Chili Con Queso Soup

Hadassah Cheese Soufflé

Lorrie Guttman
Food Editor, *Tallahassee Democrat*, Tallahassee, Florida

This recipe got its name from Hadassah, the Women's Zionist Organization of America. My mother, who lives in Tampa, is a member, as am I. She made this casserole for a Hadassah luncheon, and when it was a hit, passed along the recipe to me. I submitted it to a cookbook I helped edit, Knishes, Gefilte Fishes and Other Jewish Dishes, *for the Temple Israel Sisterhood here in Tallahassee. One of the virtues of this dish is that it can be prepared ahead, leaving only the baking on the day of serving.*

Makes 6 to 8 serving

1 pound pasteurized process cheese spread (such as Velveeta)
3 tablespoons grated sharp Cheddar cheese
1/2 cup margarine
6 eggs
1 cup milk
10 slices white bread, crusts removed
1/2 teaspoon salt
1/2 teaspoon baking powder
Ground black pepper, to taste

The day before: Melt cheese spread, Cheddar cheese and ma garine in the top of a double boiler over simmering water.

In a large bowl, beat eggs and milk. Add bread to egg mixtur then add melted cheese mixture. Stir to mix thoroughly. Add sal baking powder and pepper.

Pour mixture into a lightly greased 13x9x2-inch baking dis Allow to set overnight in the refrigerator.

The next day: Bake in a preheated 350-degree oven for 35 to 4 minutes.

Some Like It Hot Brunch Casserole

Beth Whitley Duke
Food Editor, *Amarillo Globe-News*, Amarillo, Texas

This recipe, originally published in a Bisquick cookbook, called for mozzarella cheese, mushrooms and tomatoes. My family prefers a spicier dish, so I substituted hot sausage for the regular variety, Monterey Jack for the mozzarella, chili peppers for the mushrooms and picante sauce for the tomatoes. The new version resembles the old in appearance, but the taste of the new is much zippier. We enjoy it for brunch with a side serving of picante sauce and chips, guacamole salad and maybe some warmed flour tortillas instead of bread.

Makes 8 servings

1 pound hot pork sausage, cooked and drained
2 cans (4 ounces each) diced green chilies, drained
1/2 cup sliced green onions (including green tops)
2 cups grated Monterey Jack cheese (or Cheddar cheese)
1/3 cup picante sauce (mild, medium or hot, according to taste)
1-1/4 cups buttermilk baking mix
1 cup milk
6 eggs
Salt and black pepper, to taste

Spray a 13x9x2-inch baking dish with non-stick spray. Layer cooked sausage, chilies, green onions, cheese and picante sauce in dish.

In a mixing bowl, combine baking mix, milk, eggs, salt and pepper. Gently pour over layered mixture in dish. Bake in a preheated 350-degree oven 30 minutes, or until brown.

Egg Casserole

Teri Grimes
Food Editor, *The Bradenton Herald*, Bradenton, Florida

Egg casserole might sound bizarre to most people, but when I go home for the holidays, my mother always makes this comforting dish for me. When I was a child, it was one of the few ways anyone could get me to eat eggs. Now it's a part of all my holiday gatherings, too.

Makes 8 servin

- 1/2 cup chopped onion
- 2 tablespoons butter or margarine
- 2 tablespoons all-purpose flour
- 1-1/4 cups milk
- 1 cup shredded sharp Cheddar cheese
- 6 hard-cooked eggs, peeled an sliced or quartered
- 1-1/2 cups crushed potato chip
- 10 to 12 slices bacon, fried cris and crumbled

In a large skillet, cook onion in butter until tender, but not brow Blend in flour. Add milk and cook, stirring constantly, until mixtu thickens. Add cheese; stir until melted.

Arrange half the egg slices in the bottom of a lightly grease 10x6x1-1/2-inch baking dish. Cover with half the cheese sauce, ha the potato chips and half the crumbled bacon. Repeat layers.

Bake in a preheated 350-degree oven for 30 minutes, or until h and bubbly.

Crab Cheese Fondue

Leona Carlson
Food Writer, *Rockford Register Star*, Rockford, Illinois

Don't be misled by the title. This dish is meant to be savored with a fork, not dunked with a chunk of bread. A college friend, Wilda Hughes of Pebble Beach, California, served this recipe to me about 25 years after we were graduated. It has been my favorite luncheon or late-night after-theater supper dish ever since.

Makes 5 to 6 servings

4 slices stale bread
Butter
3/4 pound Cheddar cheese
1 can (6 to 7-1/2 ounces) crab meat
3 eggs
1 cup milk
1/2 teaspoon brown sugar
1/8 teaspoon ground black pepper
1/4 teaspoon dry mustard
1/4 teaspoon salt
1/4 teaspoon seasoned salt
1/2 teaspoon instant minced onion (or 1 small green onion, chopped)
1/4 teaspoon Worcestershire sauce
1/4 teaspoon paprika

The day before: Remove crusts from bread; discard crusts or save for another use. Butter each slice of bread, then cut into very small cubes. Place half the bread cubes in the bottom of a greased 10x6x1-1/2-inch baking dish.

Grate cheese. Drain and flake crab meat. Sprinkle half the cheese on top of bread in dish; top with half the crab. Repeat layers of bread, cheese and crab.

Beat eggs in a medium mixing bowl. Add milk, brown sugar, pepper, dry mustard, salt, seasoned salt, onion, Worcestershire sauce and paprika; mix well.

Pour milk mixture over mixture in dish. Refrigerate overnight.

The next day: Bake in a preheated 300-degree oven 1-1/2 hours.

Note: This is particularly good served with tomatoes vinaigrette or pickled mushrooms; asparagus or broccoli, steamed tender-crisp; and hot rolls or garlic bread.

Christmas Brunch

Monetta L. Horr
Food Editor, *Jackson Citizen Patriot*, Jackson, Michigan

This egg dish has been called Christmas Brunch in my family for years because we have traditionally served it mid-way in opening our presents on Christmas morning. We also serve it during the year, but it still has a special place on Christmas. The Old English cheese gives it a nice flavor because it has a little more zip than Cheddar cheese. This dish is handy for special occasions because you assemble it the night before and then just pop it into the oven.

Makes 6 serving

- 8 slices white bread
- 1 package (8 ounces) Old English pasteurized process American cheese slices
- 1/4 cup margarine or butter, melted
- 3 eggs
- 1 teaspoon salt, or to taste
- 3/4 teaspoon dry mustard
- 1/2 teaspoon black pepper
- 2 cups milk

Trim crusts from bread; discard crusts or save for other uses. Cu bread into 1-inch squares. Cut the cheese slices into bite-size pieces

In a greased 2-quart casserole dish, alternate layers of bread an cheese. Pour melted margarine over the layers.

Beat eggs; stir in salt, dry mustard, pepper and milk. Combin thoroughly.

Pour egg mixture over bread-cheese layers. Cover and refrigerat overnight.

Bake, covered, in a preheated 350-degree oven for 30 minutes Uncover and bake 30 minutes, or until casserole is golden and puffy

Quiche Roquefort a la Canyon

Teri Grimes
Food Editor, *The Bradenton Herald*, Bradenton, Florida

Any discussion of one-dish meals would be incomplete without including quiche. Oh, sure, people like to say quiche is passe, but check out the luncheon menu of most restaurants and chances are there will be a quiche of the day. I really like this recipe because I'm crazy about Roquefort cheese. This recipe also is great to serve my vegetarian friends for brunch — I just leave out the bacon.

Makes 6 to 8 servings

- 4 ounces Roquefort or blue cheese
- 2 cups dairy sour cream
- 1/4 pound bacon
- 2 tablespoons butter
- 1 small onion, peeled and minced
- 2 large fresh mushrooms, chopped
- 1/4 teaspoon garlic salt
- Pinch of ground mace
- Pinch of ground black pepper
- 3 eggs, well beaten
- 1 tablespoon cornstarch
- 1 (9-inch) unbaked pie crust or puff pastry crust

In a small bowl, mash Roquefort cheese with a fork. Add sour cream; mix well. Set aside.

In a skillet, fry bacon until crisp; drain on paper towels. Crumble bacon and set aside.

Melt butter in the skillet used to fry bacon. Add onion and mushrooms; saute until softened. Stir in Roquefort mixture. Add garlic salt, mace and pepper; mix well. In a medium bowl, beat eggs with cornstarch. Stir eggs into Roquefort mixture.

Sprinkle reserved bacon in pie shell. Pour egg-cheese mixture into pie shell. Bake in a preheated 400-degree oven for 25 to 30 minutes, or until firm. Serve warm.

California Frittata

Miriam Morgan
Food Editor, *San Mateo Times,* San Mateo, California

Frittata is simply a baked omelet, and "simply" really is the proper word. Just blend the ingredients, pour them into a baking dish and put it in the oven.

The virtues of this frittata are many. It can be mixed ahead, then baked just before serving. Or, it can be baked ahead and eaten at room temperature. Serving is simple, because it is cut into squares.

This casserole makes a wonderful luncheon entree for guests or an easy dinner entree for your family. Children generally enjoy it, and it's a great way to get them to eat vegetables. I like it best when made with broccoli, but for variety I have made it with spinach and with mushrooms.

Accompany the frittata with sliced fresh fruit or fruit salad and French bread, breadsticks or muffins.

Makes 6 servings

- 3/4 to 1 pound fresh broccoli, or 1 package (10 ounces) frozen chopped broccoli
- 2 tablespoons margarine or butter
- 3 eggs
- 1 cup low-fat milk
- 1 cup all-purpose flour
- 1 teaspoon baking powder
- 1-1/2 to 2 cups shredded Cheddar cheese
- 1/4 cup grated Parmesan cheese

Wash the broccoli. Cut heads from stalks and separate into small florets. Peel the stalks, if necessary, and cut into small pieces. Blanch broccoli in rapidly boiling water, uncovered, about 5 minutes, or until barely cooked. Drain, then plunge into ice water to stop cooking and set color. Dry, then chop fine. If using frozen broccoli, simply thaw and squeeze dry.

Melt margarine in a 13x9x2-inch baking dish. Tilt pan to coat bottom. Set aside.

In a large mixing bowl, beat eggs until well combined. Add milk and beat again. Add flour, baking powder and Cheddar cheese; stir to combine. Add broccoli; stir to combine well.

Transfer batter to prepared baking dish; smooth top with a spatula, then sprinkle with Parmesan cheese. (Frittata can be prepared ahead to this point, then refrigerated, covered, up to 8 hours before baking.)

Bake in a preheated 350-degree oven for 50 to 60 minutes, or until golden brown on top.

Remove pan from oven; cool at least 10 minutes before cutting into squares to serve. Serve hot or at room temperature.

Note: Refrigerate any leftovers. Leftovers can be reheated easily in a microwave oven or toaster oven.

Spinach Frittata: Omit broccoli. Substitute 1 bunch fresh spinach, washed, dried and chopped (but uncooked). Or, use 1 package (10 ounces) frozen chopped spinach, thawed and squeezed dry.

Mushroom Frittata: Omit broccoli. Slice 1 pound fresh mushrooms; saute in 2 tablespoons olive oil, margarine or butter until limp and liquid has evaporated. Season with a sprinkling of thyme, if desired. Replace grated Cheddar cheese with Monterey Jack or Jarlsberg cheese, if desired.

Cheese-Rice Casserole

Lorrie Guttman

Food Editor, *Tallahassee Democrat*, Tallahassee, Florida

I have always thought that carrots and cheese are a great flavor combination. The sweetness of raisins (I prefer golden raisins) makes the delicious duo a tremendous trio.

Makes 6 servings

1/2 cup rice, uncooked
3 cups grated or finely shredded carrots (6 large)
2 eggs, slightly beaten
1/2 cup evaporated milk
1-1/2 teaspoons salt, or to taste
1/2 teaspoon ground black pepper
1 small onion, peeled and grated
1-1/2 cups diced pasteurized process American cheese
1/2 cup golden raisins
3/4 cup soft bread crumbs
2 tablespoons margarine, melted

Cook rice according to package directions, but do not use salt.

In a large mixing bowl, combine cooked rice, carrots, eggs, evaporated milk, salt, pepper, onion, cheese and raisins; mix well. Turn into a greased, shallow 2-quart baking dish.

In a small bowl, combine bread crumbs and margarine; toss. Sprinkle crumbs over casserole. Bake in a preheated 350-degree oven for 45 minutes, or until hot and bubbly.

Chili Con Queso Soup

Sara Anne Corrigan
Food Editor, *The Evansville Press,* Evansville, Indiana

This is not a recipe for calorie counters. We only serve it for special occasions — such as when we are hungry! It is also a good company dish because the recipe can be doubled or tripled easily.

Because this soup is so rich and filling, I generally serve it with just a fresh fruit salad, featuring citrus fruits and bananas.

The recipe comes from a former associate at the newspaper, Rick Barter, who clipped it out of an upscale food magazine some years ago.

Makes 2 servings

- 1 small onion, peeled and finely chopped (about 1/2 cup)
- 1-1/2 tablespoons butter
- 1 can (4 ounces) mild green chilies, drained, seeded and chopped
- 1 can (14 ounces) plum tomatoes, drained, seeded and chopped
- 1 package (3 ounces) cream cheese, cubed
- 1/2 cup chicken broth
- 3/4 cup half-and-half or light cream
- 2 teaspoons fresh lemon juice, or to taste
- Cayenne pepper, to taste
- Salt, to taste
- Tortilla chips, salsa and guacamole

In a large saucepan, cook onion in butter until soft. Add chilies and tomatoes. Cook 10 minutes, stirring, until liquid evaporates. Stir in cream cheese. When cream cheese has melted, add broth, half-and-half, lemon juice and cayenne. Add salt to taste. Cover and heat to serving temperature; do not boil.

Serve soup with tortilla chips, salsa and guacamole.

Rice and Noodles

98 Pizza Soup

99 Wild Rice-Beef Casserole

100 Chicken Italian

101 Wild Rice-Pecan Casserole

102 Spaghetti Pie

103 Rice and Cabbage Casserole

104 Tofu Lasagna

105 Bundt Noodle Kugel

106 Beef Stroganoff with a Difference

107 Vermicelli Soup

108 Italian Sausage and Green Beans with Pasta

109 Schinkenfleckel

110 Savory Chicken Tarragon

Pizza Soup

Jim Hillibish
Food Editor, *The Repository*, Canton, Ohio

This soup just happened one night. The family room was filled at suppertime with kids salivating for homemade pizza. They begged, they cajoled, they even offered to do the dishes. That did it. The cook of the house began assembling the usual pizza ingredients, but there was no yeast for the dough and it was too late to drive to the store. Pizza soup resulted. The kids never missed the crust.

Makes 4 serving

3/4 cup riso or acini di pepe soup macaroni, uncooked
3/4 cup chopped onion
1 cup sliced fresh mushrooms
1/4 cup chopped green bell pepper
2 cloves garlic, peeled and minced
1 teaspoon olive oil
2 cups beef broth
2 cups tomato sauce
2 teaspoons dried basil
1 teaspoon ground fennel
2 ounces mozzarella cheese, shredded
Dried basil, for garnish

In a large pot, cook macaroni in boiling water about 10 minutes, o until tender; drain.

Saute onion, mushrooms, green pepper and garlic in olive oil unti onion is transparent. Add beef broth, tomato sauce, basil, fennel an cooked macaroni; simmer 10 minutes. Mixture will thicken. Ad water to achieve desired consistency.

Ladle soup into bowls. Top each serving with 1/4 of the chees and a pinch of basil.

Note: This soup freezes well.

Wild Rice-Beef Casserole

Ann C. Wells
Food Editor, *The Grand Rapids Press*, Grand Rapids, Michigan

Wild rice is expensive, but this is an excellent way to stretch a half-pound of this delicate treat from Minnesota. It's a great family meal because it can be made ahead and will keep in the refrigerator before and after cooking.

Makes 6 to 8 servings

package (8 ounces) wild rice (see note)
cups boiling water
-1/2 pounds lean ground beef
/4 cup chopped onion
tablespoon vegetable oil (optional)
can (4 ounces) mushroom stems and pieces, drained
2 cans (10-1/2 ounces each) condensed chicken with rice soup, undiluted
1/4 teaspoon onion salt
1/4 teaspoon garlic powder
1/4 teaspoon curry powder
1/4 teaspoon soy sauce

Rinse rice; drain. Place rice in a large mixing bowl; pour boiling ater over rice. Cover and let stand for 15 minutes.

Brown ground beef and onion in a large non-stick pan or in 1 ablespoon vegetable oil in pan. Drain any fat. Transfer meat mixture ɔ a 2-quart casserole dish with a cover. Drain rice; add to meat ιixture. Add mushrooms, soup, onion salt, garlic powder, curry owder and soy sauce; mix well. Adjust seasonings, if needed. (At this oint, casserole can be refrigerated up to 2 days before baking. Or, unaked casserole can be frozen.)

Bake, covered, in a preheated 350-degree oven for 1 hour, or until ot and bubbly.

Note: For a more economical version of this casserole, substitute ne 6-ounce package long-grain and wild rice mix (such as Uncle en's) for the wild rice. Save the seasoning packet in the rice mix to eason long-grain or brown rice some other time.

Chicken Italian

Barbara Mihalevich Arciero
Food Writer, *The Times*, Shreveport, Louisiana

Robyn Rice, the woman who gave me this recipe, is an excellent cook who now lives in Edwardsville, Illinois. She's one of those cooks who has probably never experienced the trauma of flat biscuits or scorched potatoes—she's that good! I like her recipe for Italian chicken much better than the traditional Cacciatore. I usually serve it with a green salad and garlic bread.

Makes 5 to 6 servin

5 to 6 chicken breast halves
2 cans or jars (about 13 ounces each) Italian-style spaghetti sauce
1/2 cup chopped celery
1 can (16 ounces) Italian plum tomatoes, undrained, cut into small pieces
1/4 cup chopped green bell pepper
1/4 cup chopped green onion
Garlic salt, to taste
1/4 cup green olives, cut in halves
1-1/2 cups sliced fresh mushrooms
1 box (16 ounces) rigatoni noodles
2 tablespoons olive oil
2 cups grated mozzarella cheese

Boil chicken until done. (Begin preparing sauce and cooki noodles while chicken is boiling.) Let chicken cool enough to hand then remove meat from bones. Discard skin. Keep meat warm. Sa broth for another use.

While chicken is cooking, prepare sauce. In a large saucepa combine spaghetti sauce, celery, tomatoes with their liquid, gre pepper, green onion, garlic salt and green olives; simmer 20 minut Add mushrooms during the last 6 minutes of cooking.

Meanwhile, cook noodles according to package directions, addi oil to water. Drain noodles.

Place hot chicken pieces and drained, cooked noodles on a lar platter. Sprinkle mozzarella cheese over chicken and noodles. Po sauce over all.

Wild Rice-Pecan Casserole

Leona Carlson
Food Writer, *Rockford Register Star*, Rockford, Illinois

This casserole is expensive—but it's easy to prepare and is guaranteed to win you a berth in the gourmet-cook category. Serve it with poultry, pork, beef, veal, lamb, seafood or even a casserole, such as chicken and mushrooms. It gives any entree an air of elegance. It refrigerates or freezes and reheats like new.

Makes 8 servings

- 1/2 cup butter or margarine
- 1/2 pound fresh mushrooms, sliced
- 1 onion, peeled and chopped
- 2 tablespoons chopped green bell pepper
- 1 clove garlic, peeled and minced
- 1 cup chopped pecans
- 1 cup wild rice, uncooked
- 3 cups chicken broth, undiluted
- Salt and black pepper, to taste

Melt butter in a large skillet; add mushrooms, onion, green pepper and garlic. Cook 5 minutes. Add pecans. Cook 1 minute. Rinse and drain rice; mix rice into mushroom mixture. Add broth. Season to taste with salt and pepper.

Turn mixture into a well-greased 2-quart flat casserole dish. Cover. Bake in a preheated 350-degree oven 1 hour. This dish holds well in a warm oven, or it can be refrigerated and reheated.

Spaghetti Pie

Monetta L. Horr
Food Editor, *Jackson Citizen Patriot*, Jackson, Michigan

This dish is similar to lasagna but it is also a lot like spaghetti. It doesn't take a lot of exotic ingredients, and it doesn't require as much preparation as lasagna. Ground turkey can be substituted for ground beef.

Makes 4 to 6 servings

- 6 ounces spaghetti, uncooked
- 2 tablespoons margarine or butter
- 1/3 cup grated Parmesan cheese
- 2 eggs, well beaten
- 1 cup cottage cheese or ricotta cheese
- 1 pound lean ground beef (or raw ground turkey)
- 1/2 cup chopped onion
- 1/4 cup chopped green bell pepper
- 1 can (8 ounces) stewed tomatoes, undrained, chopped
- 1 can (6 ounces) tomato paste
- 1 teaspoon granulated sugar
- 1 teaspoon dried oregano
- 1/2 teaspoon garlic salt
- 1/2 cup shredded mozzarella cheese

Cook spaghetti according to package directions; drain. Stir margarine, Parmesan cheese and eggs into cooked spaghetti. Spoon mixture into a buttered 9-inch pie plate, pressing to form a "crust." Spread cottage cheese over crust.

Meanwhile, brown beef in a large skillet; drain fat. Stir in onion, green pepper, tomatoes and their liquid, tomato paste, sugar, oregano and garlic salt. Pour meat mixture over cottage cheese in crust.

Bake in a preheated 350-degree oven for 30 minutes. Sprinkle mozzarella cheese on top. Bake 5 minutes, or until cheese is melted.

Rice and Cabbage Casserole

Betty W. Bernard
Food Editor, *Lake Charles American Press*, Lake Charles, Louisiana

Nettie Cardenas, a member of the American Press *news staff, is a good cook who also has a green thumb when it comes to growing vegetables and flowers. This recipe of hers, which is also one of my favorites, makes use of cabbage that grows abundantly in gardens in southwest Louisiana.*

Makes 6 servings

- 1 small head of cabbage, washed, drained and coarsely shredded
- 2 tablespoons vegetable oil
- 3/4 cup water, divided
- 1 pound lean ground beef
- 1/2 cup finely chopped onion
- 1/4 cup finely chopped green bell pepper
- 1/4 cup finely chopped celery
- 1/4 teaspoon ground black pepper
- 1 teaspoon salt, or to taste
- Dash of garlic powder
- 3 cups cooked rice
- 1 can (8 ounces) tomato sauce
- 3/4 cup shredded Cheddar or Monterey Jack cheese
- 1/2 cup cracker crumbs or fine dry bread crumbs
- 1/2 cup cooked, crumbled bacon

In a large saucepot or Dutch oven, steam cabbage in oil and 1/4 cup water for 15 minutes. Drain and set aside.

In a large skillet, lightly brown ground beef; drain off fat. Add onion, green pepper, celery, black pepper, salt and garlic powder; mix well. Continue cooking a few minutes until vegetables are tender.

Layer steamed cabbage, cooked rice and browned meat mixture in a lightly greased 13x9x2-inch baking dish. Pour tomato sauce and remaining 1/2 cup water over all. Top with shredded cheese, cracker crumbs and crumbled bacon.

Bake, covered, in a preheated 325-degree oven for 20 minutes, or until hot and bubbly. (Or, simmer, covered, on top of stove for 20 minutes.)

Note: This can be prepared ahead of time and reheated.

Tofu Lasagna

Miriam Morgan
Food Editor, *San Mateo Times*, San Mateo, California

Lasagna is a rich dish, but this vegetarian version uses tofu to replace some of the cheese and reduce the saturated fat and cholesterol content. Spinach raises the casserole's nutrient content, making this lasagna extremely nourishing.

If your family isn't hooked on tofu, keep its presence a secret. I've served this popular dish dozens of times, and no one has ever guessed tofu is the source of its creamy texture.

Makes 6 servings

12 lasagna noodles, uncooked
2 packages (10 ounces each) frozen chopped spinach, thawed
1/2 pound firm tofu
1 cup part-skim ricotta cheese or low-fat cottage cheese
3 tablespoons olive oil
1 medium onion, peeled and chopped
3 tablespoons minced fresh parsley
2 large cloves garlic, peeled and pressed
1 can (16 ounces) tomato sauce
1 can (6 ounces) tomato paste
1 cup water
1 teaspoon honey
3/4 teaspoon crushed dried basil
3/4 teaspoon crushed dried oregano
Salt and black pepper, to taste
2 cups shredded mozzarella cheese
2/3 cup grated Parmesan cheese

Cook noodles in boiling water according to package directions. Drain carefully and set aside in a single layer on paper towels.

Squeeze spinach as dry as possible; set aside.

In a medium mixing bowl, crumble tofu and blend it with ricotta cheese until smooth and creamy.

For sauce, heat oil in a large skillet. Saute onion, parsley and garlic in oil. Add tomato sauce, tomato paste, water, honey, basil, oregano, salt and pepper. Simmer, partly covered, about 20 minutes, or until thickened.

To assemble lasagna, ladle about 2 tablespoons sauce into bottom of an 11x8x3-inch baking dish. Arrange 6 noodles to cover the bottom of the dish. Top with spinach, tofu mixture, shredded mozzarella and half the remaining sauce in that order.

Cover with remaining 6 noodles, then top with remaining sauce. Sprinkle with Parmesan cheese. Cover with foil. (Dish can be prepared ahead to this point and refrigerated until ready to bake. Add 15 minutes to baking time.)

Bake in a preheated 350-degree oven 40 minutes. Remove foil; continue baking 15 to 20 minutes, or until bubbling and crusty on top.

Remove from oven and let cool 10 minutes before cutting into squares to serve.

Note: Recipe easily can be doubled; use a larger pan or two of the same size.

Bundt Noodle Kugel

Norma Schonwetter
Syndicated Columnist, *Micro Magic*, Oak Park, Michigan

This recipe originated in a community cookbook, called Fiddler in the Kitchen, *which I edited. The recipe became a family favorite, and now my son prepares it when he needs to take a dish to a potluck gathering.*

Makes 12 servings

1/2 cup butter or margarine, melted, divided
3/4 cup firmly packed dark brown sugar
1 cup chopped walnuts
1 teaspoon salt, or to taste
4 eggs, beaten
1/2 teaspoon ground cinnamon
2/3 cup granulated sugar
1 cup dairy sour cream
3/4 cup applesauce
1 package (16 ounces) medium egg noodles, cooked and drained

Spray a 12-cup Bundt pan with non-stick vegetable spray, then pour 1/4 cup melted butter into pan. Sprinkle brown sugar evenly over butter in pan, then sprinkle chopped walnuts over brown sugar.

In a large mixing bowl, combine remaining 1/4 cup melted butter, salt, eggs, cinnamon, granulated sugar, sour cream and applesauce. Stir in cooked and drained noodles; mix well.

Turn mixture into prepared pan; bake in a preheated 350-degree oven for 1 hour, or until brown. Remove from oven; turn upside down on serving plate. Remove Bundt pan. Serve hot.

Beef Stroganoff with a Difference

Lori Longbotham
Food Editor, *New York Post*, New York City, New York

This delicious Stroganoff is made with ground beef rather than the traditional costly beef tenderloin. Since the vegetable is cooked along with the egg noodles, this entire meal can go from the skillet to the table in about 35 minutes.

Makes 4 serving

- 1 pound lean ground beef
- 1 tablespoon vegetable oil
- 1 tablespoon unsalted butter or margarine
- 2 medium onions, peeled and diced
- 2 shallots, peeled and minced
- 1/4 pound fresh mushroom caps, sliced
- 1 tablespoon minced fresh tarragon or 1 teaspoon dried tarragon
- 1/2 cup beef broth
- 1 teaspoon Dijon-style mustard
- 1/4 teaspoon freshly ground black pepper
- 4 ounces medium egg noodles, uncooked
- 1 small zucchini, grated
- Salt and black pepper, to taste
- 1/4 cup dairy sour cream or light sour cream
- 1 tablespoon minced fresh chives

Shape beef into oval patties, about 4x3x3/4 inches. Heat oil and butter in a large, heavy-bottomed skillet over medium heat. Add beef patties and cook 4 to 5 minutes on each side for medium rare. Remove with a spatula and keep warm.

Add onions and shallots to drippings in skillet. Cook 2 to 3 minutes, stirring occasionally, until browned. Stir in mushrooms; cook 2 minutes, stirring frequently, until soft. Add tarragon, broth, mustard and 1/4 teaspoon pepper; cook 2 minutes.

Meanwhile, cook noodles according to package directions; add grated zucchini 30 seconds before draining the noodles. Drain noodles and zucchini. Season to taste with salt and pepper. Keep warm.

Remove mushroom mixture from heat; add sour cream and mix well. Taste and adjust seasoning, if necessary.

Place cooked noodles and zucchini on a platter; top with beef patties. Spoon mushroom sauce over all. Garnish with chives. Serve hot.

Vermicelli Soup

Sara Anne Corrigan
Food Editor, *The Evansville Press*, Evansville, Indiana

The following recipe came in the mail to me at my office. It was part of a complete menu that "by making use of convenient canned goods," the promoters claimed, could be table ready in about 30 minutes.

The other recipes in the ensemble were forgettable, but I really liked the soup, which I now serve with crusty black bread and whatever kind of cheese I happen to have in the refrigerator at the time.

I embellished the original recipe by adding sliced fresh mushrooms. You can use common, white button mushrooms, but this soup will accommodate shiitake, or other darker, more flavorful varieties.

The soup also is forgiving when it comes to substituting ingredients or adjusting the volume of any specific item. It also microwaves nicely for a next-day lunch at the office.

Makes 6 servings

2/3 cup vermicelli or similar thin-strand pasta, broken into 1- to 2-inch pieces, uncooked
3 tablespoons vegetable oil
1/2 medium onion, peeled and chopped (about 3/4 cup)
2 large cloves garlic, peeled and minced or pressed
1 can (10-3/4 ounces) peas and carrots, drained
1 can (8 ounces) stewed tomatoes, undrained
1 can (4 ounces) diced green chilies, drained
1 can (48 to 49-1/2 ounces) chicken broth (or about 6 cups broth made from bouillon)
1 cup (or more, as desired) thinly sliced fresh mushrooms
Minced fresh parsley, for garnish

In a soup pot or Dutch oven, brown vermicelli in hot oil. Add onion and garlic; saute until onion is tender. Add peas and carrots, tomatoes with their liquid, green chilies, chicken broth and mushrooms. Cover and simmer 10 minutes. Garnish each serving with parsley.

Italian Sausage and Green Beans with Pasta

Miriam Morgan
Food Editor, *San Mateo Times,* San Mateo, California

Savory Italian sausage, which is widely available in supermarkets, flavors this hearty pasta supper. The sausage is teamed with fresh green beans and sweet bell peppers in a fragrant tomato sauce. Serve the sauce atop fettuccine and complete the meal with garlic bread and a piquant salad of sturdy greens.

Note that no extra oil or salt is added. If the sausages are drained well after browning, fat content is kept to a minimum.

Makes 4 to 6 servings

1 pound Italian sausage (mild or spicy, or a combination)
1 large yellow onion
1 green or yellow bell pepper
1 can (28 ounces) Italian-style plum tomatoes
1 pound fresh green beans
About 1/3 cup water, if needed
2 to 3 tablespoons tomato paste (optional)
1 package (12 to 16 ounces) fettuccine or wide egg noodles

Cut Italian sausage into slices about 1/2-inch thick. Peel onion and slice into rings. Place sausages and onion in a large, wide, heavy-bottomed skillet; cook over medium heat, stirring with a wooden spoon, until sausage is browned and onion rings are limp. Drain off fat from pan and discard.

While sausages and onions are cooking, slice bell pepper into strips about 1/2-inch wide. Drain tomatoes, reserving liquid. Using kitchen shears, cut tomatoes into small pieces.

After draining fat from pan, add pepper strips, tomatoes and about half the tomato liquid to the pan. Cook, uncovered, over medium heat about 5 minutes, or until sauce begins to thicken.

Snap off ends of green beans; snap beans into 2- or 3-inch lengths. Add green beans to pan; stir a few times to combine ingredients. Add remaining tomato liquid. Cover and cook over low to medium heat about 15 minutes, or until beans are tender but still somewhat firm to the bite, stirring occasionally. If more liquid is needed, add up to 1/3 cup water. If a thicker sauce is desired, stir tomato paste into sauce at he end of the cooking time. The sauce can be held on the stove, covered, with heat turned off, for several minutes, if necessary.

While sauce is cooking, bring large pot of water to boil; cook pasta according to package directions. (If fettuccine is used, break strands n half before cooking for easier eating.) When pasta is done, drain nto a colander; use some of the hot cooking water to warm a large serving bowl. Drain the bowl, then add pasta and top with sauce. Use wo large forks to toss. Serve at once.

Schinkenfleckel

Barbara Bloch
President, *International Cookbook Services*, White Plains, New York

Although my grandmother was born in Pennsylvania, she took my father and his sisters and brother to Vienna, Austria, in the early 1900s to study music. She learned how to prepare this casserole while she was in Vienna, which is why she used the German name for the recipe. Simply translated, it is Ham and Noodle Casserole — easy to make and delicious to eat.

Makes 8 servings

- 1 package (8 ounces) egg noodles, cooked and drained
- 1/2 pound cooked ham, ground
- 1 cup cottage cheese
- 1 cup dairy sour cream
- 2 eggs, beaten
- 1 teaspoon Worcestershire sauce
- Salt and freshly ground black pepper, to taste
- 1/2 cup grated Parmesan cheese

In a large mixing bowl, combine cooked noodles, ground ham, cottage cheese, sour cream, eggs, Worcestershire sauce, salt and pepper. Stir gently until well mixed. Spoon noodle mixture into a lightly greased 2-quart casserole dish. Sprinkle Parmesan cheese on top. Bake in a preheated 350-degree oven 20 to 25 minutes, or until heated through.

Savory Chicken Tarragon

Judy Johnson
Food Editor, *Mississippi Press*, Pascagoula, Mississippi

In 1989 I attended the National Chicken Cooking Contest in Hershey, Pennsylvania. At one of the meals, the Hershey Pasta Group teamed up with the National Broiler Council to present this delectable entree. I brought the recipe home, and it has since become a favorite at my family's table.

Makes 6 servin

1/4 cup margarine or butter
1/2 cup sliced onion
2 cloves garlic, peeled and minced
1-1/2 cups diced, cooked chicken (about 1 pound boneless chicken)
1-1/2 cups sliced carrots
1/3 cup chopped fresh parsley
3/4 teaspoon dried tarragon leaves
1/4 teaspoon ground black pepper
2-1/2 cups plus 2 tablespoons water, divided
1-3/4 cups chicken broth (homemade or one 14-1/2-ounce can)
1-3/4 teaspoons lemon juice
3 cups pasta (rotini, twirls or curly-roni), uncooked (8 ounces)
2 tablespoons all-purpose flour

Melt margarine in a 4-quart saucepan; add onion and garlic an saute for 1 minute. Add chicken, carrots, parsley, tarragon and peppe cook until chicken is lightly browned.

Add 2-1/2 cups water, chicken broth and lemon juice; bring to rapid boil. Stir in pasta; boil, uncovered, stirring occasionally, 1 minutes, or until pasta is tender.

Reduce heat. Blend flour with remaining 2 tablespoons wate gradually add flour mixture to chicken mixture, stirring until mixtur is smooth and thickened. Serve hot.

Beans and Legumes

112 Greek-Style Bean Soup
113 Beans and Stuff
114 Pinto Bean Casserole
115 Red Beans and Rice
116 Beans Beverly
117 Peanut Soup
118 Split Pea Soup

Greek-Style Bean Soup

Sara Anne Corrigan
Food Editor, *The Evansville Press*, Evansville, Indiana

I grew up in New England, where there remains a rich multi-cultural heritage from which to pick and choose—be it people, art, music, literature or food. When it comes to cultural gifts from the Greeks, it just doesn't get much better than the cuisine.

The following recipe, complete with serving suggestions, has been with me for nearly 20 years, dating back to my New England youth as a hippie, earth-mother vegetarian. Back then I made this recipe without the beef bouillon cubes. Ironically, many of the old stand-bys from that era have turned out to be the stuff of heart-healthy diets.

Makes 6 servings

1 pound dried black-eyed peas or navy or pea beans
2 large carrots, peeled and diced
1 large onion, peeled and finely chopped (about 1-1/2 cups)
1 cup finely chopped celery
2 large cloves garlic, peeled and minced
1 teaspoon dried mint leaves
2 bay leaves
1 tablespoon chopped fresh parsley
1/2 teaspoon fines herbes (available in supermarket spice section)
1/2 cup extra-virgin olive oil
1 can (8 ounces) tomato sauce
2 beef bouillon cubes
Salt and black pepper, to taste

Soak beans overnight in enough water to cover. Rinse well, drain and set aside.

In a large soup pot, saute carrots, onion, celery, garlic, mint, bay leaves, parsley and fines herbes in olive oil until onion is golden brown. Add tomato sauce, reserved beans and enough water to cover beans. Stir in bouillon cubes. Bring to a boil, lower heat and simmer, covered, for 1 hour, or until beans are tender. Add more water as necessary to keep beans covered. Season to taste with salt and pepper.

Serve soup as a main course with pita bread and a salad platter of sliced tomatoes, sliced raw onions and feta cheese sprinkled with olive oil, vinegar and oregano. Salad can be stuffed into pita bread, if desired.

Beans and Stuff

Barbara Mihalevich Arciero
Food Writer, *The Times*, Shreveport, Louisiana

Air Force wives have a tendency to pick up recipes from all over the world—or at least the United States. Well, I'm no exception. This side-dish recipe comes from an Alabama woman I met while my husband was stationed in Oklahoma. (That was before Louisiana, after Colorado!) This casserole is an unusual alternative to baked beans, and I have yet to find anyone who doesn't like it. It's particularly good with hamburgers, hot dogs or chicken fresh off the grill.

Makes 10 to 12 servings

- 1 can (15 ounces) pork and beans, partly drained
- 1 can (15 ounces) whole-kernel corn, drained
- 1 can (15 ounces) red kidney beans, drained
- 1 can (15 ounces) chili, with or without beans
- 3 slices bacon
- 1/2 small onion, chopped
- 1/4 green bell pepper, chopped
- 1/2 cup ketchup
- Few dashes Worcestershire sauce

In a large bowl, combine pork and beans, corn, kidney beans and chili; set aside.

In a large skillet, fry bacon until crisp. Remove from pan and drain on paper towels. When bacon is cool, crumble into small pieces. Set aside.

Saute onion and green pepper in bacon drippings. Add onion mixture and crumbled bacon to bean mixture. Stir in ketchup and Worcestershire sauce.

Pour mixture into a 4-quart casserole dish; cover. Bake in a preheated 350-degree oven for 50 to 60 minutes.

Pinto Bean Casserole

Mattie Smith-Colin
Food Editor, *Chicago Defender*, Chicago, Illinois

My husband, Robert, got this recipe from his mother, Sarah Horton Colin, who is a creative cook. Robert, in his version of the recipe, uses a food processor to chop the bell peppers and garlic. He also added a yellow bell pepper. Mother Colin only used green and red bell peppers, and she chopped them by hand. Either way, this casserole is delicious.

Makes 8 serving

- 1 pound dried pinto beans
- Water
- 1/4 pound lean ham, cubed
- 1 cup chicken broth
- 1 large yellow bell pepper, seeded and coarsely chopped
- 1 large red bell pepper, seeded and coarsely chopped
- 1 large green bell pepper, seeded and coarsely chopped
- 4 large cloves garlic, peeled and finely chopped
- 2 teaspoons cayenne pepper
- 1 tablespoon honey

Soak beans overnight in water to cover. Rinse beans, then plac them in a 4-quart saucepot and cover again with water. Cook ove high heat until water boils rapidly. Drain beans into a colander; rins thoroughly with cold water.

Wash pot to remove all starch accumulated on sides. Retur thoroughly rinsed beans to clean pot; add 5 cups cold water and ham Simmer over low heat 1-1/2 hours. Add chicken broth, bell peppers garlic and cayenne pepper. Simmer 20 minutes, or until beans ar tender. Gently stir in honey.

Pour bean mixture into a buttered 3-quart casserole dish. Bake i a preheated 325-degree oven 12 minutes.

Red Beans and Rice

Mary Denise Scourtes
Food Writer, *The Tampa Tribune*, Tampa, Florida

No Southern pantry is complete without beans and rice, and no cook worth his salt is ever without these ingredients. Red Beans and Rice has traditionally been a Louisiana custom for Monday suppers; Monday used to be known as wash day. The dish didn't need a lot of attention, and it often used leftover ham hocks or sausage from Sunday dinner. It still makes an easy, economical recipe to prepare today.

Makes 6 servings

2 cups cooked pinto beans or canned red kidney beans
4 cups water, divided
1 cup chopped onion
1 cup chopped green bell pepper
3 cloves garlic, peeled and minced
3/4 teaspoon dried oregano
1/2 teaspoon dried thyme
1 teaspoon ground black pepper
1/2 teaspoon crushed red pepper
1 bay leaf
1/2 pound cooked, drained Italian sausage, chopped
1/2 teaspoon hot pepper sauce
2 cups rice, uncooked
Fresh parsley sprigs, for garnish (optional)

Place beans, 2 cups water, onion, bell pepper and garlic in a large saucepot or Dutch oven; bring to a boil. Reduce heat to medium. Cook, uncovered, stirring occasionally, for 30 minutes. Add oregano, thyme, black pepper, red pepper, bay leaf, sausage and remaining 2 cups water. Cook 30 minutes.

Remove and discard bay leaf. Add hot pepper sauce. Stir in rice. Cook 30 minutes, or until rice is tender. Garnish with parsley, if desired.

Beans Beverly

Paul Grondahl
Features Writer, *Albany Times Union,* Albany, New York

When editors and reporters go looking for answers at the newspaper, they invariably end up turning to Beverly Massa. She's part secretary, part office manager, part nurse and part mother presence to the editorial staff.

Beverly often brings in snacks, always keeps the candy jar on her desk well stocked and doesn't mind telling a reporter who subsists on doughnuts and black coffee that he's not eating properly.

For more years than she cares to remember, Beverly has been the glue that holds the editorial department together. It seems entirely appropriate, then, that she should have passed around the newsroom this down-home, old-fashioned, rib-stickin' bean dish. In her honor, we named the dish Beans Beverly.

Makes 12 servings

- 1 pound, or less, lean ground beef
- 1/2 pound bacon, cut into pieces
- 1 cup chopped onion
- 1 clove garlic, peeled and minced
- 1/2 cup ketchup
- 1 teaspoon dry mustard
- 1 can (28 to 31 ounces) pork and beans, undrained
- 1 can (15 ounces) red kidney beans, undrained
- 1 can (15 ounces) lima beans, undrained
- 1 can (15 ounces) small butter beans, undrained
- 1/2 cup firmly packed light brown sugar
- 2 tablespoons vinegar
- 1 teaspoon salt, or to taste
- 1/4 teaspoon ground black pepper

In a large saucepot or Dutch oven, saute ground beef, bacon, onion and garlic. Add ketchup, dry mustard, pork and beans, kidney beans, lima beans, butter beans, brown sugar, vinegar, salt and pepper; mix thoroughly. Pour mixture into a large bean pot or other casserole dish. Bake in a preheated 350-degree oven about 1 hour, or until thickened.

Note: 1 can (15 ounces) black-eyed peas or other beans, undrained, can be added to the mixture.

Peanut Soup

Toni Burks
Food Editor, *Roanoke Times & World-News*, Roanoke, Virginia

Since 1882, the Hotel Roanoke has been a stately reminder of Southern hospitality. On the occasion of its 100th anniversary, the hotel published a souvenir collection of 13 of the most requested recipes in the hotel's history, Our Most Requested Recipes 1882-1982. *The hotel credits one of its early chefs with creating this regional specialty. Peanut soup makes a tasty first course for Thanksgiving dinner.*

Makes about 20 (1/2-cup) servings

1/2 cup butter
1 small onion, diced
2 ribs celery, diced
3 tablespoons all-purpose flour
2 quarts chicken broth
1 jar (16 ounces) creamy peanut butter
1 teaspoon celery salt
1 teaspoon salt, or to taste
1 tablespoon lemon juice
1/2 cup ground peanuts

Melt butter in a large saucepot or Dutch oven. Add onion and celery; saute 5 minutes, or until tender, but not browned. Add flour and mix well. In another saucepan, heat chicken broth. Gradually stir hot broth into vegetable mixture. Cook 30 minutes.

Remove from heat; strain. Add peanut butter, celery salt, salt and lemon juice to strained mixture; mix well to soften peanut butter and make a smooth soup. Return to heat briefly to warm soup. Sprinkle ground peanuts on soup just before serving.

Split Pea Soup

Carolyn Flournoy
Food Columnist, *The Times*, Shreveport, Louisiana

I worked on this recipe for five years—just to get the perfect marriage of ingredients. With the ham and sausage, you have a complete meal. My kids used to like to have cheese toast with it. It is, of course, the perfect ending for a whole or half ham. I slice the smoked sausage into one-inch pieces and steam it with 1/2 cup water to degrease it before adding it to the soup.

Makes 3 quarts; 10 to 12 servin

1 pound dried split peas
10 cups water, divided
2 celery tops, whole
1 small onion, whole
1 clove garlic, peeled and crushed
1 ham bone with some fat
1/4 teaspoon dried thyme
1/4 teaspoon hot pepper sauce
1 teaspoon granulated sugar
4 green onions, sliced (with tops)
3 ribs celery, sliced
4 carrots, peeled and sliced
2 teaspoons chicken bouillon granules
2 tablespoons lemon juice
2 cups coarsely chopped baked ham
1 pound smoked sausage, cut into 1-inch slices

In a large soup pot or Dutch oven, soak rinsed peas in 2 cups co water for 1 to 2 hours. Add remaining 8 cups water, celery tops, onio garlic and ham bone. Simmer 2 hours. Remove and discard celer onion and ham bone.

Add thyme, hot pepper sauce, sugar, green onions, sliced celer carrots, chicken bouillon granules and lemon juice. Stir well. Simm for 30 minutes. Add ham and sausage; simmer 30 to 45 minutes. Serv hot

Note: This soup can be frozen.

Vegetables

120 Quick Tomato-Pepper Gazpacho
121 Dilled Zucchini Bake
122 Pumpkin Soup with Basil
123 Country Fare Spuds
124 Imambildi
125 Cucumber Mushroom Soup
126 Spicy Broccoli Casserole
127 Vegetable Pie
128 Zucchini-Spinach Casserole
129 Spicy Baked Ratatouille
130 Squash Soup
131 Baked Potato Soup
132 Tortilla Soup
133 Steamed Red Potatoes
134 Potato Soup with Rivels
135 Delta Cabbage Soup
136 French Onion Soup
137 Celery Casserole
138 Potato Soup Base
139 Creamy Broccoli Soup
139 Herbed Cheese Soup
140 Zucchini Casserole
141 Cauliflower-Garlic Soup
142 Curried Tomato Soup
143 Okra-Tomato Bake
144 Garden Casserole
145 Red Pepper Vichyssoise
146 Cream of Corn Soup
147 Cream of Breadfruit Soup
148 Creamy Wild Rice Soup
149 Spoon Bread
150 Broccoli Noodle Bake
151 Tasty No-Brainer Soup
152 Chilled Blueberry Soup
153 Pepper Pudding
154 Avocado Zucchini Soup

Quick Tomato-Pepper Gazpacho

Anne Byrn
Food Editor, *Atlanta Journal-Constitution*, Atlanta, Georgia

During the summer months in Georgia, home-grown tomatoes get thick on the vine. We remedy this by turning them into soups, salads and other dishes. A favorite soup is gazpacho, which is made with staple provisions. Either serve this soup coarse and chunky or puree it in a blender to make a smooth soup.

Makes 6 to 8 serving

1/2 cup diced celery
1/4 cup diced green bell pepper
1/4 cup diced red bell pepper
1/2 cup diced Spanish onion
1/2 cup peeled, seeded and diced cucumber
1 cup peeled, diced fresh tomato
1 quart tomato juice
2 tablespoons red wine vinegar
2 tablespoons olive oil
1 small clove garlic, peeled an minced
1/4 teaspoon salt
1/8 teaspoon black pepper
1 teaspoon Worcestershire sauce, or more, to taste
Dairy sour cream and cucumbe slices, for garnish

In a large bowl, combine celery, green pepper, red pepper, onior cucumber, tomato, tomato juice, vinegar, olive oil, garlic, salt, blac pepper and Worcestershire sauce; mix well. (If you want a smoot soup, puree mixture in batches in an electric blender until smooth. Cover and refrigerate at least 4 hours. Stir gently before serving Garnish each serving with sour cream and cucumber slices.

Dilled Zucchini Bake

Toni Burks
Food Editor, *Roanoke Times & World-News*, Roanoke, Virginia

What home gardener doesn't have a bumper crop of zucchini? Even people who don't garden seem to acquire enough of the long, green squash to get through the summer—but not without begging for new ways to fix it. This light vegetable dish is a delicious change of taste from the usual squash-and-soup casseroles, and it's a wonderful way to show off fresh dill and chives.

Makes 6 to 8 servings

- 3 cups coarsely grated zucchini, drained well
- 3 eggs, well beaten
- 1/2 cup minced green onions (including green tops)
- 2 cloves garlic, peeled and minced
- 1/2 cup freshly grated Parmesan cheese
- 1/2 cup buttermilk baking mix
- 1 teaspoon chopped fresh dill
- 1 teaspoon chopped fresh chives
- 1 teaspoon salt, or to taste
- 1 teaspoon black pepper
- 2 tablespoons vegetable oil
- Additional grated Parmesan cheese

Combine zucchini, eggs, green onions, garlic, 1/2 cup Parmesan cheese, baking mix, dill, chives, salt, pepper and oil. Turn mixture into a lightly oiled 13x9x2-inch baking dish.

Bake in a preheated 350-degree oven for 30 minutes, or until browned. Remove from oven and sprinkle with additional Parmesan cheese.

Pumpkin Soup with Basil

Sara Anne Corrigan
Food Editor, *The Evansville Press,* Evansville, Indiana

Prior to judging a cooking contest sponsored by our newspaper several years ago, I never once had considered the pumpkin as anything other than a sculptural medium for Halloween artists and the stuff of Thanksgiving pies and breads.

This soup recipe was submitted in that contest by a woman who said that she got the recipe while visiting Ottawa, Canada, where it is a popular autumn dish. I was a little skeptical about the combination of ingredients until I tasted it. I have been serving it ever since.

Ironically, I have since found other pumpkin soup recipes but none of them has come close to matching this one for flavor and ease of preparation. I especially enjoy serving it for company in a hollowed-out cooked pumpkin "tureen."

Makes 6 servings

- 1 large yellow onion, peeled and finely minced
- 1/4 cup butter or margarine
- 1/2 pound fresh tomatoes, peeled, seeded and coarsely chopped
- 1/2 pound carrots, peeled and cut into large chunks
- 3-3/4 cups chicken broth, divided
- 1 can (16 ounces) solid-pack pumpkin
- Salt and freshly ground black pepper, to taste
- Pinch of granulated sugar
- 2 tablespoons minced fresh basil (or 1 tablespoon dried)
- 3 tablespoons heavy cream (optional)
- Grated Swiss cheese, for garnish
- Toasted curried pumpkin seeds (see note) or croutons, for garnish (optional)

In a large soup pot, saute onion in butter for 4 to 5 minutes. Add tomatoes; simmer gently for 5 to 6 minutes, or until tomatoes become slightly mushy.

In another saucepan, simmer carrots in 2-1/2 cups chicken broth, until soft. Combine cooked carrots, hot broth and pumpkin in a blender or food processor; puree until smooth, adding the remaining 1-1/4 cups chicken stock as necessary to achieve a thin, creamy consistency.

Add pumpkin mixture to onions and tomatoes in soup pot. Season ith salt, pepper, sugar and basil. Fold in heavy cream. Heat to erving temperature, but do not boil.

Pour soup into tureen. Top with grated Swiss cheese and toasted umpkin seeds or croutons, if desired.

Note: To toast pumpkin seeds, rub a little vegetable oil on your ands, then rub 1 cup hulled pumpkin seeds in hands to coat seeds ightly with oil. Place seeds on a cookie sheet. Bake in a preheated 75-degree oven 15 minutes, shaking pan occasionally. Season seeds ith salt and curry powder to taste; toss to mix well. Bake another minutes, or until crisp and golden brown.

Country Fare Spuds

Betty W. Bernard

Food Editor, *Lake Charles American Press*, Lake Charles, Louisiana

If you're having a barbecue, try this south Louisiana specialty. It's inexpensive, quick and easy to prepare, and is guaranteed to please a crowd.

Makes 8 servings

- 1 package (8-serving size) instant mashed potatoes
- 1 package (8 ounces) cream cheese, softened
- 1/3 cup chopped onion
- 1 egg, beaten
- Salt and black pepper, to taste

Prepare mashed potatoes according to package directions, reducng water to 2-1/4 cups and omitting salt.

Blend cream cheese into hot mashed potatoes. Add onion, egg, salt and pepper; mix well. Transfer to a lightly greased 1-1/2-quart casserole dish. Bake in a preheated 350-degree oven for 45 minutes.

Note: This dish freezes well, so it can be assembled and frozen before baking. Let thaw in refrigerator before baking.

Imambildi

Jim Hillibish
Food Editor, *The Repository*, Canton, Ohio

The arrival of the first eggplants in northern Ohio gardens means Imambildi time. This legendary casserole, handed down from numerous Greek and Turkish families in the area, remains a hearty favorite for a meatless main course. The name means "the holy man fainted" because the eggplant was so good.

Makes 4 main-course servin

- 2 medium eggplants
- 4 green onions (including green tops), chopped
- 6 cloves garlic, peeled and minced
- 1 cup chopped celery, including some leaves
- 2 medium tomatoes, chopped
- 1 green bell pepper, seeded and chopped
- 1/2 teaspoon crumbled bay leaves
- 1/2 teaspoon dried oregano
- 1 teaspoon dried mint
- 3 tablespoons diced fresh parsley
- 1/4 cup olive oil, divided
- 1 cup chicken broth
- Freshly ground black pepper
- Calamata olives (optional)
- Feta cheese (optional)

Peel eggplants lengthwise, leaving 1-inch bands of peel. Halv eggplants lengthwise. Scoop out the centers to make boats.

Chop scooped-out eggplant pulp; put in a large mixing bowl. Ad green onions, garlic, celery, tomatoes, green pepper, bay leave oregano, mint and parsley; mix well.

Stuff the eggplant boats with mixture. Sprinkle with a little oliv oil. Place boats in a baking dish. Pour chicken broth and remainin olive oil into dish, around the boats. Cover and bake in a preheate 325-degree oven for 45 minutes, or until eggplant is tender.

Garnish with freshly ground black pepper, Calamata olives an feta cheese.

Note: This dish does not freeze well.

Cucumber Mushroom Soup

Jim Hillibish
Food Editor, *The Repository*, Canton, Ohio

This Chinese-style soup is a light and delicate course to begin an elegant meal. Because few people have ever eaten cooked cucumbers, it offers a surprise for your guests. As for the cooking time, it takes but 15 minutes from slicing to serving. If desired, the soup can be made ahead and reheated just before serving. The soup goes exceptionally well with a board of warm Brie cheese and chilled grapes.

Makes 6 servings

- 4 cups fresh chicken broth, degreased
- 2 large cucumbers
- 1/4 pound fresh mushrooms
- 4 green onions
- 6 fresh basil leaves, for garnish

In a large saucepan, heat broth to boiling. Meanwhile, peel, quarter and seed cucumbers; cut crosswise with a sharp knife into pieces 1/8-inch wide. Make a small cut in the top of each piece. (This makes for faster cooking.) Clean and thinly slice mushrooms. Dice green onions, including green tops.

Cook cucumbers and mushrooms in broth for 8 minutes, or until cucumbers are slightly tender. Just before serving, add green onions. Pour soup into small bowls. Float a basil leaf on each serving.

Note: Freezing this soup is not recommended.

Spicy Broccoli Casserole

Janet Geissler Watson
Food Editor, *Lansing State Journal*, Lansing, Michigan

I first made this casserole to take to Thanksgiving dinner at a friend's home. Everyone agreed that it was a colorful, tasty change from plain vegetables, especially for those who like spicy dishes. When I made it a second time, I realized I had used a full teaspoon of cayenne pepper instead of the 1/4 teaspoon called for in the recipe. Both ways are delicious; feel free to adjust the spiciness to your liking.

Makes 6 to 8 servings

- 2 packages (10 ounces each) frozen chopped broccoli
- 1 jar (16 ounces) small onions, drained
- 1 can (4 ounces) whole mushrooms, drained
- 1 jar (2 ounces) chopped pimentos, drained
- 1/4 cup slivered, toasted almonds
- 1/4 to 1 teaspoon cayenne pepper, to taste
- 1 can (10-3/4 ounces) condensed cream of celery soup, undiluted
- 1 cup shredded sharp Cheddar cheese (4 ounces)

Cook broccoli according to package directions; drain. In a large mixing bowl, combine cooked broccoli, onions, mushrooms, pimentos, almonds and cayenne pepper. Pour into a greased 1-1/2-quart casserole dish. Cover with soup; top with cheese. Bake in a preheated 350-degree oven for 30 minutes.

Vegetable Pie

Barbara Bloch
President, *International Cookbook Services*, White Plains, New York

Not all pies are made with standard pie crusts. The crust for this pie is made with potatoes. You can serve it as part of a vegetarian meal or with meat, fish or poultry. Either way, it's unusual and delicious. Whenever I serve this to company, someone is sure to ask for the recipe.

Makes 6 to 8 servings

- 4 to 6 tablespoons seasoned dry bread crumbs
- 1 package (24 ounces) frozen shredded potatoes, thawed
- 1 large onion, peeled and chopped
- 2-1/2 cups shredded Swiss cheese, divided
- 4 tablespoons butter or margarine, melted
- 1 teaspoon Italian seasoning, divided
- Salt and freshly ground pepper, to taste
- 2 tablespoons olive oil
- 1 medium zucchini or 2 small yellow crookneck squash, thinly sliced
- 1/2 pound fresh mushrooms, sliced
- 3 medium tomatoes, peeled, seeded, cut into chunks
- 2 tablespoons grated Parmesan cheese

Generously butter a 10-inch pie plate or quiche dish. Sprinkle bread crumbs on bottom and up the sides of the dish. Shake out excess crumbs; set dish aside.

Combine potatoes, onion, 3/4 cup Swiss cheese, butter, 1/2 teaspoon Italian seasoning, salt and pepper in a medium mixing bowl; stir gently to mix. Spoon into pie plate and press mixture firmly on bottom and up the sides. Bake in a preheated 450-degree oven for 25 minutes.

Heat oil in a large skillet. Add zucchini, mushrooms and tomatoes. Sprinkle with remaining 1/2 teaspoon Italian seasoning, salt and pepper. Cook over moderate heat, stirring, 5 minutes.

Spoon zucchini mixture into baked crust with slotted spoon; spread evenly in crust. Sprinkle with remaining 1-3/4 cups Swiss cheese and Parmesan cheese. Bake 5 minutes, or until cheese is melted. Cut into wedges to serve.

Zucchini-Spinach Casserole

Barbara Bloch
President, *International Cookbook Services*, White Plains, New York

I have stopped growing zucchini in my garden because my neighbors and friends grow more than they can use. No one ever seems to come to my home in the fall without bringing a zucchini, or, often as not, several zucchini. Sometimes I even find zucchini left mysteriously on my back porch. This annual over-abundance of zucchini has sent me scurrying into my kitchen to find new ways to cook it. This recipe is one of my favorites.

Makes 6 serving

- 3 medium zucchini (about 2 pounds), grated
- Salt
- 4 tablespoons butter or margarine, divided
- 1 large onion, peeled and chopped
- 1 package (10 ounces) frozen chopped spinach, thawed and squeezed dry
- 1/2 teaspoon ground nutmeg
- Freshly ground pepper, to taste
- 1 cup grated Swiss or Gruyère cheese
- 1 cup dairy sour cream
- 1/4 cup seasoned dry bread crumbs
- 2 tablespoons grated Parmesan cheese

Place grated zucchini in colander, sprinkle with salt, and let stan about 45 minutes.

Melt 3 tablespoons butter in a large skillet. Add onion; cook abou 4 minutes, or until onion is translucent.

Place zucchini between several layers of paper towels and squeez out as much liquid as possible. Add drained zucchini to skillet; cook 5 minutes, stirring constantly. Add spinach, nutmeg and pepper to skillet; stir well. Cook 4 minutes. Remove skillet from heat. Stir in Swiss cheese until melted. Stir in sour cream.

Spoon mixture into a lightly greased 1-1/2-quart baking dish. Sprinkle bread crumbs and Parmesan cheese on top; dot with remaining 1 tablespoon butter. Bake, uncovered, in a preheated 350-degree oven for 25 to 30 minutes.

Spicy Baked Ratatouille

Teri Grimes
Food Editor, *The Bradenton Herald*, Bradenton, Florida

Does a cook exist who — when faced with an excess of zucchini — hasn't experimented with version after version of ratatouille? I like the following recipe because it's baked in the oven (no more endless stirring on the stove) and because the spices are a little different than more traditional versions. And don't worry about the leftovers; reheat the vegetable mixture and serve it with cooked eggs (see variation).

Makes 6 to 8 servings as a side dish; 4 as a main dish (with eggs)

teaspoons ground coriander
teaspoon ground cumin
cloves garlic, peeled and finely chopped
bay leaf, crushed
Salt and freshly ground black pepper, to taste
eggplants, unpeeled and sliced
Vegetable oil or olive oil
Chopped fresh parsley
4 zucchini, unpeeled and sliced
3 large onions, peeled and sliced
3 large green bell peppers, seeded and sliced
3 medium tomatoes, sliced or chopped

Mix coriander, cumin, garlic, bay leaf, salt and pepper in a small bowl; set seasoning mixture aside.

Put eggplant in bottom of a lightly oiled 14x11x2-inch baking dish. Sprinkle with some of the seasoning mixture, a little oil and some parsley. Top with zucchini, then onions, green peppers and tomatoes, sprinkling each layer with some of the seasoning mixture, oil and parsley.

Bake, covered, in a preheated 400-degree oven for 30 minutes. Uncover and bake for 30 minutes, or until vegetables are fork-tender. Serve hot or cold.

Variation: When vegetables are almost done, make 4 indentations in vegetable mixture. Break an egg into each indentation. Cover and cook just until eggs are set. Serve as a luncheon or supper main dish.

Squash Soup

Christine Randall

Assistant Features Editor, *Post-Courier Newspapers*, Charleston, South Caroli

I have found the perfect year-round food in this squash soup. In the winter, I eat it hot; in the summer, chilled. It's great either way. It freezes well and can be made with either yellow summer squash or zucchini. Make up a big batch and you'll be set for weeks.

Makes 10 to 12 servin

- 1/4 cup butter or margarine
- 2 tablespoons vegetable oil
- 1 large onion, peeled and minced
- 2 cloves garlic, peeled and minced
- 3 pounds yellow squash or zucchini, thinly sliced
- 3-1/2 to 4 cups chicken broth
- 1 cup half-and-half or light cream
- 1-1/2 teaspoons salt, or to taste
- 1/2 teaspoon ground black pepper

Melt butter in a Dutch oven. Add oil; mix well. Add onion an garlic; saute until tender. Stir in squash and chicken broth. Cover an simmer 15 to 20 minutes, or until squash is tender.

Spoon about one-third of the squash mixture into an electr blender or food processor; process until smooth. Repeat with remai ing squash. Return to Dutch oven.

Stir in half-and-half, salt and pepper. Cook over low heat, stirrin constantly, until well heated. Serve hot or chilled.

Baked Potato Soup

Beverly Bundy
Food Writer, *Fort Worth Star-Telegraph*, Fort Worth, Texas

One of the Fort Worth Star-Telegram*'s readers stumbled upon a wonderful soup while visiting a sick friend in the hospital. She requested the recipe in the newpaper's recipe exchange column. The food and nutrition services department of Medical City in Dallas was happy to share the recipe.*

Makes 5 cups

/4 cup instant mashed potato flakes or granules
cups chicken broth
/2 cup margarine or butter
/2 cup all-purpose flour
cups milk
large baked potatoes, with skin on, diced
1/4 teaspoon garlic powder
1/4 teaspoon ground white pepper
1/4 teaspoon granulated sugar
1/4 teaspoon ground black pepper
Salt, to taste (optional

'or toppings:
tablespoons grated Cheddar cheese
slices bacon, fried crisp and crumbled
5 tablespoons chopped fresh chives

In a medium mixing bowl, combine potato flakes with chicken roth; set aside.

Melt margarine in a medium saucepan. Add flour and cook, tirring, until flour is lightly browned. Slowly stir in milk. Cook, tirring continuously, to make a medium white sauce. Add potato-roth mixture and diced baked potatoes. Add garlic powder, white epper, sugar and black pepper. Add salt to taste. Simmer until soup s desired thickness.

Ladle soup into heated bowls. Top each serving with cheese, bacon nd chives.

Tortilla Soup

Beverly Bundy
Food Writer, *Fort Worth Star-Telegram*, Fort Worth, Texas

Biscuits, corn bread and tortillas are the breads of the Southwest. Many restaurants serve peanut butter and jelly on flour tortillas on their childrens' menus. Scrambled eggs and sausage are packed in tortillas for breakfast tacos. In this regional favorite, corn tortillas add crunch to soup.

Makes 6 to 8 servin

10 corn tortillas, cut in slivers
1/2 cup corn oil or vegetable oil, divided
4 bell peppers (any color), seeded and chopped
2 tomatoes, seeded and chopped
1 white onion, peeled and minced
1 clove garlic, peeled and minced
2 quarts chicken broth
Dash of hot pepper sauce (optional)
Salt and black pepper, to taste
3 cups shredded Cheddar cheese

In a large skillet, fry tortilla slivers in 1/4 cup oil until browne drain on paper towels. Saute bell peppers in oil remaining in skille drain on paper towels.

Add remaining 1/4 cup oil to skillet. Add tomatoes, onion ar garlic; saute until soft. Add chicken broth and bring to a boil. Seasc to taste with hot pepper sauce, salt and pepper.

Divide fried tortillas, bell peppers and shredded cheese among 6 8 large soup bowls. Pour soup into bowls and serve hot.

Steamed Red Potatoes

Mattie Smith-Colin
Food Editor, *Chicago Defender,* Chicago, Illinois

Cousin Ben's Steamed Red Potatoes are standard fare for Sunday and holiday brunches for our family when Ben is in Chicago. Ben is Judge Benjamin Travis, presiding judge of the Appellate Department, Superior Court, Alameda County, Oakland, California. He is in Chicago frequently because his wife, attorney Anne Fredd, lives in Chicago.

Cousin Ben enjoys cooking so much that he volunteers to cook the food for social events of family and friends. He says he has developed some of his best recipes while waiting for a jury to return with a verdict.

Family members report that this recipe originated in Atlanta, Georgia. The late Lessie Clarke Travis, Ben's mother, prepared Steamed Red Potatoes often for her family of nine children. Aunt Lessie cooked them in a black, cast-iron skillet; Ben uses an electric skillet.

Makes 10 generous servings

4 pounds red potatoes
6 large green bell peppers
4 large white onions
5 teaspoons virgin olive oil
1 teaspoon salt substitute (or season with salt to taste)
2 teaspoons cayenne pepper

Place potatoes in a large bowl and cover with water. Let potatoes soak while you seed and coarsely chop the green peppers, then peel and coarsely chop the onions. Remove potatoes from water and scrub. Do not peel. Cut potatoes into 1/16-inch (thin) slices.

Heat olive oil in an electric skillet or in a large, heavy skillet. Add potato slices to hot oil. Cover and let "steam." Turn occasionally with a metal spatula. When potatoes are medium brown, add green peppers, onions, salt substitute and cayenne pepper. Using a large spoon, gently stir vegetables and seasonings into potatoes. Cover. Continue to cook until potatoes are golden brown. Serve immediately.

Potato Soup with Rivels

June Ann Gladfelter
Assistant Managing Editor/Features, *The Express*, Easton, Pennsylvania

This has been my favorite "comfort food" for most of my life. We had it often when I was growing up because almost everyone in my family liked it, especially my dad. The recipe was developed by my mother, Minnie Gladfelter. Although both Mom and Dad are of Pennsylvania Dutch heritage, it was my dad who had tasted the soup and liked it. After he and Mom were married, he asked her whether she could make the soup. He told her what he thought the ingredients were, and she took it from there.

Makes 6 servings

6 medium potatoes, peeled and diced
1 quart water
1-1/4 teaspoons salt, divided (or to taste)
1 egg
1 cup all-purpose flour
2 tablespoons butter

Put potatoes, water and 1 teaspoon salt in a large pot or Dutch oven Cook about 10 minutes, or until potatoes are soft.

Meanwhile, using a fork, slightly beat egg. Work in the flour anc remaining 1/4 teaspoon salt until mixture is crumbly.

When potatoes are soft, drop in the crumbly mixture (rivels), a littl at a time, to avoid clumping, and stir. Stir in butter; cook for 6 minutes

Delta Cabbage Soup

Betty W. Bernard
Food Editor, *Lake Charles American Press*, Lake Charles, Louisiana

Because southwest Louisiana is blessed with fertile soil and mild winters, it is easy for people to have backyard gardens all year long. One winter crop is cabbage. This soup recipe, given to me by Nettie Cardenas, an American Press *staff member, makes use of this versatile vegetable.*

Makes 6 to 8 servings

3 cups chicken broth
3 cups water
1/2 cup shredded carrots
1/2 cup finely chopped celery
1 medium potato, peeled and diced
1/2 cup chopped onion
2 cups chopped, peeled fresh tomatoes
2-1/2 teaspoons salt, or to taste
1 bay leaf
4 black peppercorns
3 cups shredded cabbage
1/4 cup lemon juice
1 tablespoon granulated sugar

In a large soup kettle, combine broth, water, carrots, celery, potato, onion, tomatoes, salt, bay leaf and peppercorns.

Simmer, covered, for 1 hour, stirring occasionally. Add cabbage; simmer 10 minutes. Stir in lemon juice and sugar; cook about 1 minute, or until heated through.

French Onion Soup

Norma Schonwetter
Syndicated Columnist, *Micro Magic*, Oak Park, Michigan

I kept improvising on my recipe for French Onion Soup until I developed this one. It's as good as the best baked onion soup in any restaurant. Whenever I have a lot of onions to use up, I prepare a pot of this soup because it doesn't take long to prepare, especially when using a food processor to slice the onions. Add a salad and you have a delightful meal.

Makes 4 hearty serving

4 medium onions, peeled and thinly sliced
1/2 teaspoon granulated sugar
1/4 cup butter or margarine
2-2/3 cups strong beef broth made from instant beef bouillon granules(or two 10-1/2-ounce cans condensed beef broth, undiluted)
1 tablespoon all-purpose flour
Ground black pepper, to taste
1 teaspoon Worcestershire sauce
4 thick slices French bread, toasted
2/3 cup grated Parmesan cheese
1-1/2 cups grated Gruyère or Swiss cheese

In a large skillet, slowly cook onions in sugar and butter until sof and light brown. Add beef broth, flour, pepper and Worcestershire sauce; mix well. Cover and simmer 30 minutes.

Pour soup into individual oven-proof casserole dishes. Top each with a slice of bread. Combine Parmesan and Gruyère cheeses; divide cheese mixture among casseroles, topping bread slices. Bake in a preheated 325-degree oven for 25 minutes, then put under broiler for 1 minute to brown cheese slightly.

Celery Casserole

Lorrie Guttman

Food Editor, *Tallahassee Democrat*, Tallahassee, Florida

Celery is an underrated vegetable, generally thought of as something to munch when you're on a diet and seldom used as the main part of a dish. As this casserole shows, however, celery can be a star. This was the first-place winner in one of our newspaper's recipe contests. I have, at times, varied the dish by adding other vegetables I have on hand, such as yellow squash.

Makes 8 servings

- 3 cups diced celery
- 1/4 cup or more slivered almonds
- 1 can (8 ounces) sliced water chestnuts, drained
- 1 can (4 ounces) sliced mushrooms, drained
- 1/2 cup (8 tablespoons) butter, divided
- 3 tablespoons all-purpose flour
- 1 cup chicken broth
- 3/4 cup half-and-half or light cream
- 1/2 cup grated Parmesan cheese
- 1/2 cup soft bread crumbs
- Finely chopped fresh parsley
- Paprika

Cook celery in a small amount of boiling salted water. Drain. Combine drained celery, almonds, water chestnuts and mushrooms. Pour into a lightly greased 12x8x2-inch baking dish.

Melt 5 tablespoons butter in a large skillet, then blend in flour. Cook over low heat, stirring, until thick. Slowly add broth and half-and-half. Cook over medium heat, stirring constantly, until thick and bubbly. Pour over celery mixture.

Melt remaining 3 tablespoons butter. Combine Parmesan cheese, bread crumbs and melted butter. Sprinkle cheese-crumb mixture over top of casserole. Sprinkle with parsley and paprika. Bake in a preheated 350-degree oven for 25 minutes.

Potato Soup Base

Norma Schonwetter
Syndicated Columnist, *Micro Magic*, Oak Park, Michigan

This robust potato soup base is a cinch to prepare and it's also economical. You can use the base to prepare an endless variety of soups. Use leftover vegetables and/or meats as well as different seasonings and herbs. Here's the basic recipe with a couple of variations. I think the soup is especially easy to prepare in the microwave oven.

Makes about 2 quarts soup base, or enough for 8 serving

- 2 tablespoons butter or margarine
- 1 large onion, peeled and thinly sliced
- 5 cups hot tap water
- 2 teaspoons instant chicken bouillon granules
- 1 tablespoon dried parsley flakes
- 5 cups peeled, sliced potatoes (sliced about 1/8-inch thick)

Melt butter in a 3-quart saucepan over medium heat. Add onio and cook about 5 minutes, or until onion is soft. Add hot water bouillon granules, parsley and potatoes. Bring to a boil. Cover an simmer about 10 minutes, or until potatoes are tender. In two batches blend until smooth in an electric blender or food processor.

Use to prepare either of the following soups. Unused soup base ca be stored in the refrigerator or frozen for later use.

Microwave method: Combine butter and onion in a 3-quart microwave-safe casserole dish. Microwave, uncovered, on High (100 percent) power for 4-1/2 minutes, or until onions are tender, stirring once during cooking. Add 1 cup hot tap water, bouillon granules, parsley and potatoes; stir to mix. Cover and microwave on High power 11 minutes, stirring twice. Let stand 5 minutes.

Add 2 cups hot water; stir to mix. In two batches, blend until smooth in electric blender or food processor. Return mixture to casserole dish. Stir in remaining 2 cups hot water; mix until smooth.

Use soup base to prepare either of the following soups.

Creamy Broccoli Soup

Makes 4 servings

1 quart potato soup base (see master recipe)
1 cup cooked, pureed broccoli
1/8 teaspoon garlic powder
3/4 teaspoon celery salt
Freshly ground pepper, to taste

Combine soup base, pureed broccoli, garlic powder, celery salt and pepper in a 2-quart saucepan. Simmer about 10 minutes, or until hot.

Microwave method: In a 2-quart casserole dish, combine soup base, pureed broccoli, garlic powder, celery salt and pepper. Microwave, covered, on High (100 percent) power for 3 minutes, or until heated through.

Herbed Cheese Soup

Makes 4 servings

1 quart potato soup base (see master recipe)
1 cup finely shredded cabbage
1 cup finely shredded carrots
1/2 teaspoon salt, or to taste
1/8 teaspoon ground black pepper
1/4 cup ketchup
3/4 teaspoon dried thyme
1/4 teaspoon dried tarragon
1 cup shredded Baby Swiss, Swiss or Cheddar cheese

In a 2-quart saucepan, combine soup base, cabbage, carrots, salt, pepper, ketchup, thyme and tarragon. Bring to a boil; reduce heat and simmer 10 minutes, or until carrots are tender-crisp. Stir in cheese; heat (do not boil), stirring, until cheese has melted.

Microwave method: Pour soup base into a 2-quart casserole dish. Stir in cabbage, carrots, salt, pepper, ketchup, thyme and tarragon. Microwave, covered, on High (100 percent) power 6 minutes, stirring once. Microwave on Medium (50 percent) power for 6 minutes, or until carrots are tender-crisp. Remove soup from microwave oven. Stir in cheese while soup is hot, so cheese will melt.

Zucchini Casserole

Sara Anne Corrigan
Food Editor, *The Evansville Press*, Evansville, Indiana

The following recipe was a first-prize winner in a recipe contest sponsored by my newspaper several years ago. One of my jobs back then was to serve as a judge in this annual event, which attracted hundreds of participants from southern Indiana, western Kentucky and southern Illinois, an area we in Evansville fondly refer to as the Tri-State.

This recipe yields a dish that belies the simplicity of the ingredients and instructions. The woman who submitted it said it was a great recipe to keep on hand for picnics and church suppers where everyone has to bring a covered dish.

After a few bumper crops of zucchini (are there any other kind?) and a few potluck suppers, I tend to concur.

Please note that in the instructions, the casserole is to be baked uncovered for the first 20 minutes, then covered for the last 10 minutes, which is the opposite procedure from many casserole recipes. This, however, is not a mistake. The first 20 minutes will allow excess moisture to escape from the dish so that you will have a casserole and not a soup.

Best of all, fresh zucchini seems to be available—and cheap—all year 'round, in case your potluck supper is in February.

Makes 6 to 8 serving

- 3-1/2 cups thinly sliced fresh zucchini
- 2 small onions, peeled and sliced (about 1 cup)
- 1/2 cup butter or margarine
- 1 box (6 ounces) stovetop-style cornmeal stuffing mix
- 1 can (10-3/4 ounces) condensed cream of chicken soup, undiluted
- 1 cup dairy sour cream

Steam zucchini and onions until tender.

Meanwhile, melt butter in a large skillet. Add stuffing mix; stir to combine. Press half of the stuffing mixture into a greased 13x9x2-inch baking pan.

When zucchini and onions are tender, drain well. Add soup and sour cream to zucchini and onions; mix well. Pour zucchini mixture over stuffing mix in pan; sprinkle remaining stuffing mix evenly over the top. Bake, uncovered, in a preheated 350-degree oven for 20 minutes. Cover and bake 10 minutes longer.

Cauliflower-Garlic Soup

Lorrie Guttman

Food Editor, *Tallahassee Democrat*, Tallahassee, Florida

Garlic becomes surprisingly mellow as it cooks, and the 20 cloves in this soup are just right. I got this recipe when it was submitted for our newspaper's Capital Chef recipe contest, for which I'm the tester. The original version calls for pureeing the cooked cauliflower in a blender, but I like to simply break it up with a cooking spoon so that the soup has a more interesting texture.

Makes 6 servings

20 cloves garlic, peeled
5 cups chicken broth (homemade or canned)
1 large head cauliflower (8 cups florets)
Salt and white pepper, to taste
1 cup half-and-half or light cream
Freshly grated nutmeg

In a covered soup pot, simmer garlic in broth 20 minutes. Add cauliflower, salt and white pepper; simmer about 30 minutes, or until cauliflower is tender.

Break up cauliflower with a spoon. Taste and adjust seasonings. Stir in half-and-half. Simmer until soup reaches serving temperature. Top each serving with a grating of nutmeg.

Note: Soup can be refrigerated after adding half-and-half, for a refreshing cold soup in the summer.

Curried Tomato Soup

Sara Anne Corrigan
Food Editor, *The Evansville Press*, Evansville, Indiana

The only thing I know for sure about the origin of this recipe is that it was published in a newspaper. I know this because the tattered yellow copy I have is definitely newsprint. I have been serving it for years, not so much as a component of a meal, but as a hot beverage, as soothing in its own way as cocoa or tea.

"Soothing?" you might ask. "But it's full of curry!" That's true, but I've discovered you can control the fire, if desired.

On the other hand, if you have been outside working or playing in the snow, this soup is almost magical in its ability to warm you up. As an added benefit, it's so low in calories and fat that you can enjoy a second cup without a second thought.

Makes 2 to 3 serving

- 1 can (10-3/4 ounces) condensed cream of tomato soup, undiluted
- 1 soup can water
- 2 tablespoons dark brown sugar
- 2 tablespoons fresh lemon juic
- 1 to 2 teaspoons curry powder, to taste
- Yogurt or dairy sour cream, for garnish (optional)

In a saucepan, combine soup, water, brown sugar and lemon juice mix well. Add 1 scant teaspoon curry powder and bring mixture to boil. Taste and add more curry powder, a little at a time, until soup ha the flavor and fire you want.

Serve soup hot with a dollop of yogurt or sour cream, if desired.

Note: Soup can be reheated in the microwave oven.

Okra-Tomato Bake

Teri Grimes

Food Editor, *The Bradenton Herald*, Bradenton, Florida

Back home in Kentucky, okra is a favorite summertime food, whether sliced and fried in cornmeal, simmered whole in butter or added to a big pot of vegetable soup. Although Floridians don't seem to take to okra like the folks back home, I can get my fill of "Mom food" anytime I want with this casserole. It uses frozen okra, so it's always in season.

Makes 4 to 6 servings as a side dish

1/2 pound bacon
1 medium onion, peeled and finely chopped
1 package (10 ounces) frozen cut okra, thawed
1 small green bell pepper, finely chopped
2 tablespoons instant rice, uncooked
1 can (16 ounces) whole tomatoes, undrained
1 tablespoon granulated sugar
Dash of garlic salt
1/4 teaspoon salt
1/8 teaspoon black pepper
1 tablespoon grated Parmesan cheese
1/4 cup fine dry bread crumbs
1 tablespoon butter or margarine, melted

Cook bacon in a large skillet until crisp. Drain bacon, reserving drippings in skillet. Crumble bacon and set aside.

Cook onion and okra in reserved bacon drippings until lightly browned. Drain on paper towels. Place onion and okra in lightly greased 1-1/2-quart casserole dish. Add green pepper, rice and reserved crumbled bacon; mix well.

Combine tomatoes, sugar, garlic salt, salt and pepper in container of electric blender; blend. Pour over mixture in casserole dish. Top with Parmesan cheese. Combine bread crumbs and butter; mix well. Sprinkle on top of casserole. Bake in a preheated 350-degree oven for 45 minutes.

Garden Casserole

Monetta L. Horr
Food Editor, *Jackson Citizen Patriot*, Jackson, Michigan

This is a nutritious recipe that tastes great and uses many garden vegetables. The brown rice is nice and chewy, and the cashews add crunch. It does take 30 minutes or so of preparation time: cleaning the veggies, cutting and sauteing them. So this isn't a recipe to serve in a hurry. However, one time I made it to serve company and my guests joined me in the kitchen and helped with the preparation. We all had almost as much fun making it as we did eating it.

Makes 6 serving

2 tablespoons butter, melted
1-1/2 cups brown rice, uncooked
2 large onions, peeled and chopped, divided
3 cups chicken or beef broth
3 tablespoons soy sauce (low sodium, if desired)
1/2 teaspoon dried thyme
1 teaspoon salt, or to taste
3 tablespoons vegetable oil
2 cloves garlic, peeled and finely chopped
1 bunch broccoli, cut into florets
1 head cauliflower, cut into florets
2 red bell peppers, seeded and cut into strips
1 cup roasted, salted cashews
2 cups shredded Cheddar or Monterey Jack cheese

In a 3-quart casserole dish, mix butter, rice, half the chopped onion broth and soy sauce. Cover and bake in a preheated 350-degree over for 50 to 60 minutes, or until rice is cooked. Stir in thyme and salt.

Meanwhile, heat oil in a skillet; saute remaining onion and garlic broccoli, cauliflower and bell pepper for 5 minutes over high heat.

Pour vegetables over rice mixture. Cover. Return to oven and bake 10 minutes longer. Remove lid. Sprinkle cashews over vegetables. Mound cheese around edges. Return to oven and bake 5 minutes, or until cheese is melted.

Note: Dry roasted or unsalted cashews can be substituted for roasted, salted cashews.

Red Pepper Vichyssoise

Anne Byrn

Food Editor, *Atlanta Journal-Constitution*, Atlanta, Georgia

Mary Hataway, owner of Patio by the River restaurant in Atlanta, is always thinking up new combinations of classic dishes. Take vichyssoise. She improvises on the basic recipe by adding a puree of red peppers. It adds color and flavor. She even makes her own version of creme fraiche. This recipe has become a favorite of mine; I like to serve it at summer parties.

Makes 6 servings

2 tablespoons unsalted butter
2 cups finely sliced leeks (white part, plus tender part of green tops)
3 cups peeled, finely sliced potatoes
4-1/2 cups chicken broth
1 cup heavy cream
Salt and white pepper, to taste
2 to 3 red bell peppers, seeded and cut into thirds
Chopped fresh chives, for garnish
Creme fraiche, garnish (optional; see note)

Melt butter in a large saucepan or Dutch oven; add leeks and saute until soft. Add potatoes and broth; simmer, partly covered, until potatoes are tender, about 30 minutes.

Puree soup in blender or food processor in batches; put pureed mixture in a large mixing bowl. Add cream. Season to taste with salt and pepper.

Broil red peppers, skin-side up, about 6 minutes. Remove and discard skins, seeds and membranes. Puree pepper pulp in blender or food processor until smooth.

Stir pepper puree into soup; blend thoroughly. Refrigerate soup for 3 to 4 hours, or until well chilled.

Ladle cold soup into serving bowls. Garnish with chopped chives and a dollop of creme fraiche, if desired.

Note: Creme fraiche can be prepared by adding 2 tablespoons buttermilk to 1 cup heavy cream. Cover and let sit on counter overnight. Mixture will thicken and have a "nutty" flavor similar to French cream. Refrigerate until needed.

Cream of Corn Soup

Florence D. Roggenbach
Food Editor, *Norfolk Daily News*, Norfolk, Nebraska

My mother, Delora Holt Karella, was 16 when she was married, and knew absolutely nothing about cooking. My father, Ambrose J. Karella, was 12 years older and he taught her most of her baking skills. This soup recipe is one of my mother's.

Makes 4 serving

- 1-1/2 teaspoons minced onion
- 1 tablespoon chopped celery leaves (see note)
- 3 tablespoons butter or margarine, melted
- 3 tablespoons all-purpose flour
- 2 cups milk, scalded
- 1 cup boiling water
- 1 cup corn (fresh, frozen or canned)
- Salt and black pepper, to taste

Brown onion and celery leaves in butter. Add flour. Mix until smooth. Add scalded milk slowly, stirring constantly. Add boiling water. Cook in the top of a double boiler over hot water until thickened and smooth. Add corn. Season to taste with salt and pepper. Heat thoroughly.

Note: If desired, celery salt to taste can be substituted for chopped celery leaves.

Cream of Breadfruit Soup

Judy Johnson
Food Editor, *Mississippi Press*, Pascagoula, Mississippi

Tropical cooking is not just for us coastal folks anymore. Distributors of exotic produce are making the delicate flavors of the tropics available throughout the nation. When it comes to the islands, nothing is so typically tropical as breadfruit. Although it is native to Southeast Asia, breadfruit has become a staple of the islands of the Caribbean. Home economists at J.R. Brooks, a distributor of specialty produce, developed this recipe, and it has become one of my favorites.

Makes about 4 servings

1 average breadfruit (choose a firm, green one)
2 tablespoons butter
1/2 clove garlic, peeled and minced
1 medium onion, peeled and chopped
1 quart chicken broth
Salt and black pepper, to taste
1 cup half-and-half or light cream
Chopped fresh chives, for garnish

Cut and peel breadfruit; slice into small pieces. Discard spongy core section. Cook pieces in boiling salted water about 30 minutes, or until soft. Drain and mash as you would potatoes. You will need about 1-1/2 cups mashed breadfruit for this recipe. Set aside.

Melt butter in a large skillet. Add garlic and onion; saute until soft, but not browned. Add chicken broth and about 1-1/2 cups mashed breadfruit. Cook over medium heat, stirring often, until mixture is smooth and beginning to thicken. Season with salt and pepper.

Remove from heat. Slowly stir in half-and-half until soup is smooth and creamy. Top with chopped chives.

Note: This soup can be served warm or cold.

Creamy Wild Rice Soup

Norma Schonwetter
Syndicated Columnist, *Micro Magic*, Oak Park, Michigan

This unusual soup originally was developed by the American Dairy Association. I tasted it at a food convention and decided to adapt it for the microwave oven. It's a gourmet soup that is easy to prepare. The flavor intensifies when the soup is made a day in advance. A food processor will speed up the chopping and slicing of the vegetables for this soup.

Makes 8 servings

- 1/2 cup wild rice, uncooked
- 5 cups low-sodium chicken broth, divided
- 2 tablespoons margarine or butter
- 2 medium carrots, peeled and coarsely shredded
- 1 medium onion, peeled and finely chopped
- 2 ribs celery, finely chopped
- 1 cup sliced fresh mushrooms
- 1/4 cup all-purpose flour
- 1-1/4 cups evaporated skim milk
- 1/2 teaspoon salt, or to taste
- 1/4 teaspoon ground black pepper
- 1 teaspoon dried leaf savory
- 3 tablespoons lemon juice
- Sprigs of fresh dill, for garnish (optional)

Rinse rice; drain. Combine rice and 2 cups broth in a large saucepan. Bring to boil; cover and simmer about 1 hour, or until rice is tender. Set aside.

In a medium skillet, combine margarine, carrots, onion and celery. Cover and cook over medium heat until vegetables are soft, stirring occasionally. Add mushrooms and cook, uncovered, about 1 minute, or until mushrooms are soft. Stir in flour; gradually add remaining 3 cups broth, mixing well until smooth. Cook over medium heat, stirring constantly, until thickened. Stir in cooked rice, milk, salt, pepper and savory. Simmer until heated through, stirring occasionally. Add lemon juice; mix well. Garnish with fresh dill, if desired.

Microwave method: Rinse rice; drain. Combine rice and 2 cups broth in a 1-quart microwave-safe baking dish. Cover and microwave on High (100 percent) power 4 minutes, or until boiling. Microwave on Medium (50 percent) power for 15 to 20 minutes, or until most of the rice has burst slightly. Set aside.

Combine margarine, carrots, onion and celery in a 3-quart microwave-safe baking dish. Microwave, covered, on High power 5 minutes, or until vegetables are soft, stirring once. Add mushrooms; microwave, covered, on High 1 minute. Stir in flour. Gradually add remaining 3 cups broth, mixing well. Microwave, uncovered, on High 7 minutes, or until slightly thickened, stirring once. Stir in cooked rice, milk, salt, pepper and savory. Microwave, uncovered, on High power 6 minutes, or until heated through, stirring once. Add lemon juice; mix well. Garnish with fresh dill, if desired.

Spoon Bread

Toni Burks
Food Editor, *Roanoke Times & World-News*, Roanoke, Virginia

Spoon Bread is a fine Southern tradition—a dish rich in good corn flavor, but light with a pudding-like texture. As its name suggests, Spoon Bread is spooned out for serving because it is too moist to slice or cut. It should be served immediately upon removal from the oven. Accompany it with plenty of butter and serve it with anything that goes well with corn bread.

Note that this recipe differs from usual ones that involve blending a cooked mixture with beaten egg whites. This recipe side-steps that tedious task, but still produces a light, wonderful casserole.

Makes 4 to 6 servings

2 cups milk
1/2 cup white cornmeal
3 tablespoons butter
1/2 teaspoon salt, or to taste
3 eggs, beaten
Butter, for serving

Pour milk into a 2-quart saucepan over medium heat. Slowly stir in cornmeal. Cook, stirring occasionally, until mixture thickens. Remove from heat; add butter and salt and mix well. Allow to cool for 15 minutes.

Fold beaten eggs into cooled mixture; stir well. Pour into a greased 1-1/2-quart baking dish. Bake in a preheated 350-degree oven for 45 to 55 minutes, or until nicely puffed and the top is lightly browned.

Serve spoon bread immediately, accompanied by plenty of butter.

Broccoli Noodle Bake

Monetta L. Horr
Food Editor, *Jackson Citizen Patriot*, Jackson, Michigan

I got this recipe from a potluck at work. Before I had a chance to try it at home, our family was invited to a potluck dinner following a Brownie ceremony for our daughter, Heather. This recipe seemed like a natural, so it's what I took. When it came time to eat, I helped our 5-year-old son, A.J., with his plate and gave him a serving of the casserole. After we sat down with some new friends, A.J. kept complimenting me on the casserole, saying it was the best he had ever eaten and asking why didn't I make it more often. I'm sure people thought I was putting him up to those comments.

Makes 10 servings

1/2 cup margarine or butter
1 onion, peeled and chopped
1 green bell pepper, seeded and chopped
3 or 4 ribs celery, chopped
2 packages (10 ounces each) frozen chopped broccoli, thawed
8 ounces spaghetti, uncooked
10 to 12 ounces Cheddar cheese grated (about 2 cups), divided
2 cans (10-3/4 ounces each) condensed cream of mushroom soup, undiluted
1/2 soup can milk
1 can (4 ounces) whole or sliced mushrooms, drained

Melt margarine in a large saucepan; saute onion, green pepper and celery. Put broccoli on top; cover and simmer 5 to 10 minutes.

Meanwhile, cook spaghetti according to package directions; drain.

In a buttered 3-quart casserole dish, layer spaghetti, vegetable mixture and three-fourths of the cheese. In a small bowl, combine soup and milk; pour over mixture in dish. Spread mushrooms on top. Sprinkle remaining cheese on mushrooms. Bake in a preheated 350-degree oven 35 to 45 minutes, or until hot and bubbling.

Tasty No-Brainer Soup

Carolyn Flournoy
Food Columnist, *The Times,* Shreveport, Louisiana

Perhaps my favorite hobby (or avocation) is playing duplicate/tournament bridge, which has a vocabulary of its own. If a hand is so simple that a 4-year-old could make the contract, it's called a "no-brainer." Over the years, I've dubbed certain recipes "no-brainers" — those using mixes, partly prepared food, canned soup, etc. They're invariably my readers' favorites. This soup recipe was given to me by a friend who got it from a friend, neither of whom consider themselves cooks.

Makes 8 to 10 servings

3 ribs celery, chopped
3 carrots, peeled and chopped
1 onion, peeled and chopped
1/4 cup butter or margarine
2 cans (10-3/4 ounces each) cream of potato soup, undiluted
2 cans (14-1/2 ounces each) chicken broth
1 pound pasteurized process cheese spread (such as Velveeta), cut into cubes
1 carton (16 ounces) dairy sour cream

In a large saucepot with a heavy bottom, saute celery, carrots and onion in butter for 20 to 25 minutes over very low heat. Add potato soup and chicken broth; mix well. Cover and simmer 1 hour. Add cheese spread and sour cream; let simmer 10 minutes, but do not boil.

Note: This soup is good served in hollowed-out rolls.

Chilled Blueberry Soup

Anne Byrn

Food Editor, *Atlanta Journal-Constitution*, Atlanta, Georgia

Kay Goldstein, a talented Atlanta cook, developed this recipe for her restaurant, Pentimento, in the Woodruff Arts Center. People frequent the restaurant before or after viewing an art exhibit, so the food also has visual appeal. Almost any fresh fruit can be substituted for blueberries in this recipe, but I like using our locally grown Georgia blueberries, which are so plentiful in the summer months.

Makes 6 to 8 serving

About 1 pound fresh blueberries
4 cups heavy cream, divided
1/3 cup raspberry vinegar
1/3 cup honey
Mint leaves, for garnish (optional)

Rinse and drain blueberries. Measure 14 ounces to use in soup reserve other berries for garnish. Puree 14 ounces blueberries i blender or food processor. Add 1 cup cream and raspberry vinegar process to blend.

In a medium saucepan, heat honey and remaining 3 cups cream over medium heat. Combine honey mixture with blueberry mixture refrigerate until well chilled.

Serve cold soup garnished with reserved blueberries and min leaves, if desired.

Pepper Pudding

Toni Burks
Food Editor, *Roanoke Times & World-News,* Roanoke, Virginia

Good cooks not only know how to use a pinch of this and a pat of that to the best advantage, they also know what ingredients complement each other no matter how unlikely the combination. For example, one cook I know added chopped green peppers, fresh tomatoes, crackers and cheese to her usual corn pudding to create what she calls pepper pudding. When canned hominy is substituted for the corn and some cumin and garlic powder are added, the dish takes on a completely new character, but it's still called pepper pudding.

Makes 6 to 8 servings

- 2 large green bell peppers, seeded and diced
- 2 large red-ripe tomatoes, diced
- 1 can (14-1/2 or 15-1/2 ounces) golden hominy, drained
- 2 cups coarse saltine cracker crumbs
- 2 cups grated sharp Cheddar cheese
- 1/4 cup butter or margarine
- 2 cups half-and-half or light cream
- 2 eggs, beaten
- 1 teaspoon ground cumin
- 1/2 teaspoon garlic powder
- 1/4 teaspoon red pepper flakes
- 1/2 teaspoon salt

Generously butter a 2-quart baking dish. Arrange alternating layers of green peppers, tomatoes, hominy, cracker crumbs and cheese in dish, dotting each layer with a bit of butter.

Combine half-and-half, eggs, cumin, garlic powder, red pepper flakes and salt. Pour egg mixture over ingredients in baking dish. Use a knife to cut through mixture to allow some of the egg mixture to seep in.

Bake in a preheated 350-degree oven for 45 minutes to 1 hour, or until custard is set and the pudding is browned on top.

Avocado Zucchini Soup

Sara Anne Corrigan
Food Editor, *The Evansville Press*, Evansville, Indiana

I have a hard time selling the notion of a cold soup here in the Midwest. I do, however, understand people's reluctance to try something that, to them, sounds like a non sequitur.

My family, on the other hand, relishes the thought of cool soups on hot Southern Indiana nights. I have a large collection of such soups; this one is among our favorites —and it's not just because we are inundated with zucchini every summer. This soup makes an especially nice first course with a grilled chicken dinner.

Makes 4 to 6 servings

- 1 cup diced zucchini, well drained
- 1 cup chicken broth
- 1 soft, ripe avocado, pitted, peeled and cut into chunks
- 1/4 cup minced onion
- 1-1/2 cups dairy sour cream or plain yogurt, or a combination
- 1/4 cup fresh lime juice
- 1 teaspoon salt, or to taste
- 1/2 teaspoon ground white pepper
- Dash of cayenne pepper
- Diced pimento and extra slices avocado, for garnish (optional)

Combine zucchini, broth, avocado and onion in blender or food processor; puree. Stir in sour cream, lime juice, salt, white pepper and cayenne pepper. Refrigerate, covered, until thoroughly chilled.

Garnish each serving with pimento and extra slices of fresh avocado, if desired.

Index

A

ALLIGATOR
- Sauce Piquante, 55

ARTICHOKE
- Florida Paella, 74
- Oyster Soup, Back Burner, 75

ASPARAGUS
- Austrian-Style Ragout Soup with Bread Dumplings, 62
- Super Summer Chicken, 25

AVOCADO
- Zucchini Soup, 154

B

BARLEY
- Lake Erie Clipper Soup, 32

BEANS
- Beverly, 116
- Casserole, Pinto, 114
- Chili Con Carne, 41
- Frontier Stew, 36
- and Rice, Red, 115
- Soup, Greek-Style, 112
- and Stuff, 113
- Turkey Chili, 26

BEEF
- Baked Steak, 39
- Beans Beverly, 116
- Borscht, 43
- Brazilian Chuck Roast, 40
- and Cabbage, Sweet-and-Sour, 44
- Cajun Stuffed Peppers, 34
- Casserole, Wild Rice, 99
- Chile Relleno Casserole, 50
- Chili Con Carne, 41
- Frontier Stew, 36
- Great Pumpkin Meatloaf, 35
- Kohlrabi Stew, 46
- Lake Erie Clipper Soup, 32
- Mid-Eastern Lamb-Stuffed Eggplant, 53
- Moussaka, 42
- Nutty Noodle Casserole, 37
- Oven Stew, 47
- Rice and Cabbage Casserole, 103
- Southern Pot Roast, 33
- Spaghetti Pie, 102
- Stifado, 49
- Stroganoff with a Difference, 106
- Sukiyaki, 45
- Swedish Meat Soup, 38
- Uruguayan-Style Meat Pie, 48

BEETS
- Borscht, 43

BLUEBERRIES
- Soup, Chilled, 152

BREAD
- Spoon, 149

BREADFRUIT
- Soup, Cream of, 147

BROCCOLI
- California Frittata, 94
- Casserole, Spicy, 126
- Garden Casserole, 144
- Noodle Bake, 150
- Soup, Creamy, 139

C

CABBAGE
- Beef Sukiyaki, 45
- and Beef, Sweet-and-Sour, 44
- Borscht, 43
- and Rice Casserole, 103

Soup, Delta, 135
CARROTS
Cheese-Rice Casserole, 95
Tasty No-Brainer Soup, 151
CATFISH
Caribbean, 83
CAULIFLOWER
Garden Casserole, 144
Garlic Soup, 141
CELERY
Casserole, 137
CHEESE
California Frittata, 94
Christmas Brunch, 92
Fondue, Crab, 91
Quiche Roquefort a la
Canyon, 93
Rice Casserole, 95
Soufflé, Hadassah, 88
Soup, Herbed, 139
Tortilla Soup, 132
CHICKEN
Breasts with Tomatoes and
Shiitake Mushrooms, 27
Casserole, 29
and Dumplings, Zesty, 18
Florida Paella, 74
and Grits, Gourmet, 17
Italian, 100
New Mexican Enchilada
Casserole, 20
with Orange-Nut Rice, Baked, 19
Pie, Jenny's, 30
Pie, Self-Crust, 16
Sausage and Rice Casserole, 28
South American, 24
Super Summer, 25
Tarragon, Savory, 110
Working Mom's Stew, 23
CHILIES
Casserole, Relleno, 50
Con Queso Soup, 96
Pork, Green, 58
Some Like It Hot Brunch
Casserole, 89
Vermicelli Soup, 107
CHIPS
Egg Casserole, 90
New Mexican Enchilada
Casserole, 20
CLAMS
Chowder, Buttermilk Bay, 78
COD
Portuguese-Style Boatman's
Stew, 86
Thick and Hearty Fish Soup, 79
COFFEE
Brazilian Chuck Roast, 40
CORN
Beans and Stuff, 113
Frogmore Stew, 81
Soup, Cream of, 146
CORNMEAL
Spoon Bread, 149
COUSCOUS
Chicken Breasts with Tomatoes
and Shiitake Mushrooms, 27
CRAB
Cheese Fondue, 91
Creole Seafood Supreme, 70
Royale, 82
CRAWFISH
Casserole, Louisiana, 76
CUCUMBER
Mushroom Soup, 125

D

DUMPLINGS
with Austrian-Style Ragout
Soup, Bread, 62
and Zesty Chicken, 18

E

EGGPLANT
- Imambildi, 124
- Mid-Eastern Lamb-Stuffed, 53
- Moussaka, 42
- Spicy Baked Ratatouille, 129

EGGS
- Bundt Noodle Kugel, 105
- California Frittata, 94
- Casserole, 90
- Christmas Brunch, 92
- Quiche Roguefort a la Canyon, 93
- Some Like It Hot Brunch Casserole, 89
- Spoon Bread, 149

ENCHILADA
- Casserole, New Mexican, 20

F

FISH
- Baked Halibut with Orange and Sun-Dried Tomatoes, 73
- Catfish Carribean, 83
- Dilled Seafood Medley, 69
- Mexican-Style Snapper with Lime, 84
- Mullet Stew, 77
- Portuguese-Style Boatman's Stew, 86
- Riviera Sole, 72
- Soup, Thick and Hearty, 79
- Tin Can Casserole, 85
- Tuna Casserole, 67

FLOUNDER
- Dilled Seafood Medley, 69

FONDUE
- Crab Cheese, 91

G

GAZPACHO
- Quick Tomato-Pepper, 120

GRAPES
- Riviera Sole, 72

GREEN BEANS
- and Italian Sausage with Pasta, 108
- Jiffy Scallop Casserole, 68
- Thick and Hearty Fish Soup, 79

GRITS
- and Gourmet Chicken, 17

H-K

HAM
- Casserole, Potato, Cheddar and, 52
- Harvest Sweet Potato Meat Pie, 61
- Pinto Bean Casserole, 114
- Schinkenfleckel, 109
- Split Pea Soup, 118

KOHLRABI
- Stew, 46

L-O

LAMB
- Curry, East Indian, 54
- Stifado, 49
- Stuffed Eggplant, Mid-Eastern, 53

LEEKS
- Red Pepper Vichyssoise, 145

LIVER
- Fricassee, 57

NOODLES
Casserole, Nutty, 37
Kugel, Bundt, 105
Liver Fricassee, 57
OKRA
Tomato Bake, 143
ONION
Soup, French, 136
Stifado, 49
Swedish Meat Soup, 38
OYSTERS
He Stew, 66
Soup, Back Burner Artichoke, 75

P-Q

PASTA
Chicken Italian, 100
Creole Shrimp with Fettuccine Meunière, 80
with Italian Sausage and Green Beans, 108
Lake Erie Clipper Soup, 32
Nutty Noodle Casserole, 37
Pizza Soup, 98
Savory Chicken Tarragon, 110
Spaghetti Pie, 102
Turkey Tetrazzini, 21
Tofu Lasagna, 104
Vermicelli Soup, 107
PEANUTS
Soup, 117
PEAS
Jenny's Chicken Pie, 30
Soup, Split, 118
PEPPERS
Cajun Stuffed, 34
Garden Casserole, 144
Pudding, 153
Vichyssoise, Red, 145
PORK
Chops, Hurry-Up, 64
Chops with Three Mushrooms, Chinese-Style, 60
Green Chili, 58
POTATOES
Cheddar and Ham Casserole, 52
Country Fare Spuds, 123
Hurry-Up Pork Chops, 64
Red Pepper Vichyssoise, 145
Soup, Baked, 131
Soup Base, 138
Soup with Rivels, 134
South American Chicken, 24
Steamed Red, 133
PUDDING
Pepper, 153
PUMPKIN
Meatloaf, Great, 35
Soup with Basil, 122
QUICHE
Roquefort a la Canyon, 93

R

RICE
Alligator Sauce Piquante, 55
with Baked Chicken, Orange-Nut, 19
Beef Casserole, Wild 99
Beef Sukiyaki, 45
and Cabbage Casserole, 103
Cajun Stuffed Peppers, 34
Cheese Casserole, 95
Chicken and Sausage Casserole, 28
Crab Royale, 82
East Indian Lamb Curry, 54
Garden Casserole, 144
Louisiana Crawfish Casserole, 76
Mullet Stew, 77
Pecan Casserole, Wild, 101
and Red Beans, 115

Some Like It Hot Brunch
Casserole, 89
Soup, Creamy Wild, 148

S

SAUSAGE
Chicken and Rice Casserole, 28
Dip, 59
Florida Paella, 74
Frogmore Stew, 81
and Green Beans with Pasta,
Italian, 108
Harvest Sweet Potato Meat
Pie, 61
Red Beans and Rice, 115
Some Like It Hot Brunch
Casserole, 89
Split Pea Soup, 118
SCALLOPS
Casserole, Jiffy, 68
Dilled Seafood Medley, 69
Florida Paella, 74
SHRIMP
Barbecued, 71
Creole Seafood Supreme, 70
Dilled Seafood Medley, 69
with Fettuccine Meunière,
Creole, 80
Florida Paella, 74
Frogmore Stew, 81
SOUP
Avocado Zucchini Soup, 154
Back Burner
Artichoke-Oyster, 75
Baked Potato, 131
Base, Potato, 138
with Basil, Pumpkin, 122
with Bread Dumplings,
Austrian-Style Ragout, 62
Buttermilk Bay Clam
Chowder, 78
Cauliflower-Garlic, 141
Chili Con Queso, 96
Chilled Blueberry, 152
Cream of Breadfruit, 147
Cream of Corn, 146
Creamy Broccoli, 139
Creamy Wild Rice, 148
Cucumber Mushroom, 125
Curried Tomato, 142
Delta Cabbage, 135
French Onion, 136
Greek-Style Bean, 112
Herbed Cheese, 139
Lake Erie Clipper, 32
Meat, Swedish, 38
Peanut, 117
Pizza, 98
with Rivels, Potato, 134
Split Pea, 118
Squash, 130
Thick and Hearty Fish, 79
Tortilla, 132
Vermicelli, 107
SPINACH
Beef Sukiyaki, 45
Casserole, Zucchini, 128
Tofu Lasagna, 104
SQUASH
Soup, 130
Vegetable Pie, 127
SWEET POTATOES
Meat Pie, Harvest, 61

T-Z

TOFU
Beef Sukiyaki, 45
Lasagna, 104

TOMATOES
Bake, Okra, 143
Baked Halibut with Orange and Sun-Dried, 73
Buttermilk Bay Clam Chowder, 78
Delta Cabbage Soup, 135
Italian Sausage and Green Beans with Pasta, 108
Pepper Gazpacho, Quick, 120
Pumpkin Soup with Basil, 122
Spaghetti Pie, 102
Soup, Curried, 142
TORTILLAS
Soup, 132
Zesty Chicken and Dumplings, 18
TUNA
Casserole, 67
Tin Can Casserole, 85
TURKEY
Chili, 26
Gourmet Chicken and Grits, 17
Self-Crust Chicken Pie, 16
Sloppy Joes, 22
Spaghetti Pie, 102
Tetrazzini, 21
VEAL
Austrian-Style Ragout Soup with Bread Dumplings, 62
Stew, Tarragon, 56
ZUCCHINI
Bake, Dilled, 121
Beef Stroganoff with a Difference, 106
Casserole, 140
Soup, Avocado, 154
Spicy Baked Ratatouille, 129
Spinach Casserole, 128
Turkey Sloppy Joes, 22
Vegetable Pie, 127